D1806074

A Time to Fight

WITHDRAWN

Edited by
Dennis Pepper

NELSON

s Nelson and Sons Ltd
n Way Windmill Road
ary-on-Thames
dlesex TW16 7HP

O. Box 73146 Nairobi Kenya

.O. Box 943
95 Church Street
Kingston 5
Jamaica

Thomas Nelson (Australia) Ltd
19–39 Jeffcott Street
West Melbourne
Victoria 3003

Thomas Nelson and Sons (Canada) Ltd
81 Curlew Drive
Don Mills
Ontario

Thomas Nelson (Nigeria) Ltd
8 Ilupeju Bypass
PMB 1303 Ikeja
Lagos

Selection © Thomas Nelson and Sons Ltd 1978
First published 1978
ISBN 0 17 432088 4

Photosetting by Thomson Press (India) Limited, New Delhi
Printed and bound in Hong Kong

This collection is for Nicholas

Contents

A Wrist Watch and Some Ants

'Like to buy a wrist watch?' Robbie had said. 'Cost me six pounds—let you have it for three.'

And after the deal was settled Robbie went out on patrol, never to be seen again. A listening post heard the crack of rifle shots and the banging of grenades and that was all.

Well, it was his watch now. His thumb and forefinger pinched the smooth metal casing as he experienced all the pride of personal ownership. He liked the round, black face, the bright numerals and the white glow of the luminous hands. A fine timekeeper like this was sure to bring good fortune, and that was where Robbie made a mistake in giving it away at such a bargain price. Sheer superstition, of course, but if the watch could bring luck the proof was coming soon. The time was 0445 hours. In half an hour they would cross the start-line.

He struggled to his feet within the narrow damp walls of the slit trench and poked his head above ground level. It was dark, neither night nor morning, and the chill of the air almost set him sneezing.

Clambering out of the soft lips of the trench that crumbled under his weight, he stood up to tug off the gas-cape worn to keep out the night dew.

The outside surface of the cape was wet, and as he lay it out on the sand to roll it up, he could feel the gritty stuff clinging to it. Sand was a nuisance. When the wind blew or the shells dropped near, it went down your neck, into your eyes, nose and everything. The complaint about sand he had made in a letter home brought back a snooty reply from father, pointing out he was lucky not to slog in the mud of Flanders like the last war. There was something in this reminder. At least sand was clean.

The drumming thunder down the line had died away. Another job for the Geordies was over.

Now a new attack was starting, and a lot nearer, for he could see the spluttering gun-flashes winking like devil's eyes, and flares blazing up and sinking from their zenith, remotely, hanging low in the sky like stars. Red and green Very lights* and coloured anti-aircraft shells spangled the heaven in a crazy pattern.

The men in his platoon slept soundly in their sandpits, undisturbed by the nearness of a fierce battle. You had to snatch sleep when you could. Good luck to whoever was in the show, but it was their business. You had your own worries coming soon.

He hailed the sentry.

'Aye, it's all quiet, sir,' said Dougall.

'Good.'

On the left the guns were booming over the dark desert waste, the sky was shot with coloured tracer, and from above came the sinister organ-drone of the bombers, but there was no trace of paradoxical humour in Dougall's voice.

It stuck him as funny, and he smiled.

Sergeant Erskine was asleep when he walked over.

'Time to get ready, Sergeant! Look sharp! Waken the others in platoon headquarters. I'll do the sections myself.'

Late the previous night the battalion had stolen forward and dug in on the start-line taped by the intelligence section. His platoon of three sections lay close to the tape, fifty yards between them. The slit trenches of the sections were laid out in a blunt arrow-head, and the attack developed with the leader at the head of the centre arrow.

In the darkness beyond the white tape were the enemy lines, the attackers crossing a mile of flat open ground

*coloured flares fired from a pistol

until they reached a wadi* running diagonally across their front.

Then came the main wadi with a minefield and an anti-tank ditch behind it. After that it was close fighting, and, as the Jocks had it, 'every man for hissel'!'

The men were ready now, out of their trenches, and lying on the tape.

In front, over the ground soon to be raped by the soldiers, the milky glare of a flare-light hung in ghost-like suspension. Instinctively they hugged the ground as a shell burst noisily fifty yards in front. It came with an urgent hissing rush, ending in a sudden brevity of flame, red and fierce, and a deafening crash. Thin slivers of metal sang through the air and plopped in the sand around them.

Zwish, zwish, zwish—a fusillade of Spandau† bullets whined over their heads.

Crump! Crump! another salvo churned up the vacant space before them.

It was growing lighter. The inky blackness had turned to lilac, and the stars were waning. A faint stir of wind touched their faces. Silver bars oozed from the sun's furnace below the eastern horizon.

He could just discern the navigating party between his company and the right forward company.

His watch told him they had four minutes to go.

This waiting was a bit awkward. You wanted a cigarette badly and there was a 'no smoking' order. You wanted to rush forward wildly in a mad helter-skelter. You wanted the whole show cancelled, and an easy-going cushioned existence back home thousands of miles away.

He felt restless. He rose, and, crouching low, darted back to shake hands with the sergeant. He felt his hand tremble a little.

'Good luck, Sergeant Erskine. Don't think I'm the

*a dried-up water-course   † type of German machine-gun next to grow jittery. It's only the cold that makes me shiver.'

'Good luck, sir, and don't worry, because I'm thinking the same as you.'

He returned to the tape and lay down. His rifle and bayonet rested on the crook of his arm to keep the sand from clogging the muzzle and the breech. He ran his forefinger down the bayonet blade. It was cold and moist.

The sergeant knew what he was thinking? He wondered. And what should one think about at a time like this?

'My mother, my home, my sweetheart, good times of the past, the way Marion laughed when I tumbled into a mountain torrent in Sutherland, kilt and all? Fear of death, the supernatural, the slender promise of life after this?'

His memory served up broken fragments of the past, but somehow the lingering sentiments wouldn't fit into any prescribed pattern.

I've done this job before. Becomes almost a routine now. It's a cinch I'll be hit again. Infantry subalterns in the first lot that go over haven't much chance of coming through unhurt.

It was like this on the third night in Alamein. Told George I thought it was my turn for an iron ration, and it was.

Wasn't pleasant to hear the air hissing out of my chest, and feeling the blood gurgle in my throat when I tried to breathe. Let's hope it hits me in a safe place this time, like an arm or leg fracture.

Funny, a battlefield would be the most exciting place you could find if you knew you weren't going to be killed or maimed. It would be fun in a way to stride about with hell let loose around you, cutting a heroic figure like Errol Flynn in a movie, with maybe trickles of red-ink blood dribbling down your forehead, and your face mud-daubed by the make-up man, and showing off to the others who are

8

scared, and laughing at death-dealing bullets and flying fragments of metal.

But it doesn't work that way. Nobody can be nonchalant in attack's environment of death and mutilation. It wants every ounce of guts just to keep going and do your duty.

I know that now. I can think coldly and be calculated about it. There's no question of sentiment, self-pity or mock heroism. After you've gone through it once, it all works straight.

Even if this is an attack, it's not a piece of unthinking brutishness. Not simply rushing on and jabbing your bayonet into some poor chap. Often in peace-time you wondered just how stalwart you could be on a battlefield. This is your chance to learn now. Maybe it's worth something to a man to find that out.

As these thoughts flooded his mind and quickly ebbed, it struck him he wasn't a peace-time romancer now, but a trained soldier, conscious of his innate fears and churning them down inside of him, because he had been given orders and must carry them out. This was where military discipline counted. No room in one's head for sentiment or the melancholy burden of self-pity. He was thinking of the plan of the battle, keeping a vigilant eye on the navigating party, wondering if this or that soldier would have the guts to see it through.

It was still growing lighter. The lilac had wasted to a vapourish grey, soon to be brushed aside by the magic touch of a pink desert dawn.

Hundreds of pairs of eyes stared ahead in a vain endeavour to glimpse the evil, unseen world before them.

Suddenly the navigating party on the right rose to their feet. He grasped his rifle, and, quietly calling his men, moved forward.

They crossed the start line.

There was something weird and unworldly in the half-light about this sectional line of human arrowheads advancing slowly forward. He had seen ants, black ants of the desert, surging on to some mad purpose. He had crushed scores of them under the iron-tipped heel of his ammunition boot, unthinkingly and unfeelingly, when there wasn't much else to do. But men weren't black ants. Flesh and blood of his homeland weren't meant to lie wounded and dying out there in the desolate waste of Southern Tunisia.

Tightly he gripped his rifle, knuckles strained white, and banished the revelation to its proper place.

At the first shock of the Army's artillery barrage the desert sand shuddered beneath their feet. Vicious shells screamed over their heads and beyond. Infernally, everything vibrated to the hellish concussions.

Compass bearing of ten degrees. God, this advance is gallingly slow. One hundred yards in two and a half minutes. Like a funeral march without the hushed silence of reverence, and the music's not so sweet. Be three-quarters of an hour before we get there.

His heart was thumping; his lips were dry.

But we must keep time with the guns.

The left-hand section was straining too far ahead.

'Keep the line on the left!' he shouted above the din, and waved his arm. 'Don't bunch!'

'Keep your dressing!'

His commands seemed woefully inadequate. Surely the puny language of the parade-ground wasn't meant for so momentous an occasion as this.

'Back! Back on the right!'

Sergeant Erskine in the rear was also bawling orders.

Strange we should be yelling at them to go slower. Silly of me to doubt their courage on the start-line. But my men are tired; have been in action for weeks, with daily casualties. I can forgive myself. What men! What a grand battalion!

He glanced round quickly and saw the sergeant, cool and somehow grimly at ease, the only one of them to have the rifle slung on his shoulder, and wanting only a cigarette drooping from his lips to complete a picture of sheer self-control. He felt this man was taking it much better than himself. He waved and they both smiled, as if each was aware of a new sudden upsurge of comradeship.

'That's the stuff, you Highlanders! Come on, keep it up!'

Now the battle was raging furiously.

The battalion were forcing a bridgehead in the enemy lines and holding the breach against fire from left, right and centre. Two more Highland battalions were being thrown in later to enlarge the gap and smash through. Army artillery whammed the strong points, while a brigade on the right were firing all they had from their static positions against the enemy on that flank. Smoke shells screened the attack, confusing the enemy's direct aim. It confounded his automatic fire, for the assaulting troops could hear streams of bullets whistling overhead. Or maybe it was their own machine-guns letting loose. It wasn't easy to tell in the confusion.

But enemy guns and mortars were seeking out victims. They would walk into the hell soon.

Ahead the grey sand and gravel danced madly in incessant eruption, ravished into spouts of flaming sand and dust clouds, overhung by a long, low bank of black smoke. Above, the sky was rent by airburst cracking into snaky black streamers from which jagged metal darted downwards. Little more than a hundred yards in front bullets hissed up misty spurts of sand.

I wonder how many of my platoon will survive this racket. Christ! there's three that won't!

He saw them stagger when a shell burst in front. A cloud of smoke engulfed them. He thought the nearest one was Graham. He had dropped his rifle, clutching his chest as he swayed like an axed tree and toppled over face down.

Nobody stopped. He was glad of that. It was hard to

11

pass by wounded men, despite orders. They were all wanted forward, and stretcher-bearers would pick up the wounded later.

He found the sight ugly.

My other attacks have been at night in darkness. A bursting shell or a mine exploding then is only another bang, a flash of flame, and staccato silhouettes. But it's daylight now. You see men dropping, see their actual mutilation.

More men fell as they reached the first wadi: the ant-like figures still kept the line. Down the shallow near slope they tumbled, and climbed up the other side.

They were on ground level again. Superficially, it was quite flat, and its colour a monochrome of yellow; but they found themselves stumbling as they trampled stones, shell-holes and tiny bumps of sand crowned with sparse tufts of scrub and camel-thorn, which in the slanting rays of the morning sun stained the sand in dappled brown shadows.

It was warm in the rising sun, and the strain of the long advance was telling. It didn't seem as if the clash would ever come, this going on and on endlessly to the very dissolution of things. A trickle of sweat ran down from the padding of his steel helmet. Another sweat-drop caught in his eyelash in a tangled shot of iridescent colour.

He swerved to avoid a human leg severed above the knee. It was smooth and unmarked; the boot was there; the puttee and hose-top with a Highlander's red garter-flash. But there was no sign of the body.

At last the main wadi. As they staggered down the deep face he looked along the line. It was still straight. It was still moving on. But it was a lot thinner. There would be black crêpe hanging in many homes in the shire after this.

They were catching it hard now. All round the earth spat and mushroomed smoke and dust. The din was deafening. The enemy couldn't see what he was firing at, yet he was working accurately from map-deduced ranging. The morning air smelt of smoke and dust and cordite.

They swarmed out of the wadi, and, excitedly, he saw through the haze that they had emerged straight on to one of the gaps cleared by sappers* under cover of darkness. There was the white tape leading them through. Great stuff!

He waved wildly and the left-hand section darted for the gap. He followed on, leading the others. They were in a long single file. It was impossible to resist the urge to scurry through for fear of being caught by fire in the narrow defile.

They were through. The first section swung to the left in line again, the centre fanned out and the rear section wheeled to the right.

How splendidly the men are behaving! I'm lucky to have such grand fellows. Infantry is rough stuff, but you're dealing with men, not machines.

A fearful rushing noise like an oncoming express train, instantly followed by the inevitable bang, compelled him to turn round. As he feared, the platoon headquarters had caught it. It was a giant shell. The smoke was dense and he saw nothing in the quick rearward glance. Next it was anti-personnel mines, covered with canvas camouflage, and the men jumping hither and thither to avoid the deadly rows. Then they tumbled into the ten-foot drop of the anti-tank ditch.

He looked at his watch. Three minutes to six. The field-guns were concentrating on the ditch from then until the hour. It was easy to remember the plan now, but not in the hectic rush through the minefield.

'Stay in the ditch!' he yelled. 'Only for three minutes.'

Three minutes was like three years. It was living on the slope of a Vesuvius, a crazy row and spouts of fire spraying the men huddled low in the ditch, half burying them in showers of sand and stones. About

* Military engineers

13

half his platoon had come thus far. If one shell landed in the narrow confined walls, well . . . it wasn't a nice thought.

He pulled out a packet of army issue cigarettes from his breast pocket and offered one to Martin, who lay next to him.

'Mine's a Minor,* Martin. What's yours?' he shouted in the man's ear.

They puffed nervously at the cigarettes and studied the dial of the wrist watch.

'Like my watch, Martin?'

'It's got a bonny face, sir, but Ah wish it wis six o'clock the nicht.'

'So do I.'

Slowly the hand touched the hour. Although the bombardment of their own gunners had stopped, enemy guns were thundering, too.

'Notice any difference, Martin?'

'No verra much,' the soldier replied. His brown hair dangled askew from the helmet over his forehead. He grinned.

'Can't hear you. Shout louder.'

'Ah said not much, sir.'

'Time's up—help me.'

They stood half upright. Martin cupped his hands, and he stepped on them, pulling himself up the wall of the ditch.

Shells were dropping thickly, and the view was battle-clouded. He read the compass bearing for direction and turned round to see Bill, the company commander, jumping into the ditch.

'Wait for me!' Bill bawled.

Soon they were together, checking the bearing. The platoon on the left were already scaling the wall.

'O.K.,' Bill cried. 'By the way, your sergeant's in a bad way.'

*catch-phrase, originally an advertisement for a brand of cigarettes

14

He knew, from the way Bill said it, Erskine was dead. He shouted to his men, waited until they were beside him, and rushed forward. Now for them. His bayonet was ready.

A man on the right leaped ahead and lunged down. Another two joined him in the bloody work. Then they were all there, yelling and swearing like mad. Must be the first small post shown in the air photograph. There was a hell of a din with shells and mortar-bombs banging all over the place.

Then it came. An ear-splitting blast about four yards in front of him and he was flung backwards on the sand.

Dazedly he looked up to see Bill passing a few feet away. No good asking him to stop: he was wanted in front. Bill shouted something about 'bad luck' and 'stretcher-bearers,' then went out of sight.

He knew it was his arm. There was a burning numbness at the elbow. He was lying on his right side, supported by the haversack on his back. His left arm hung loosely, attached by only a couple of sinews from the elbow downwards. The knuckle end of a bone stuck out starkly and the rest was just a shattered bloody mess. The inside of his left boot was torn, and the foot felt warmly wet inside. His shorts were soaking and dark-stained on his right thigh.

Well, he had made a job of it this time. He lay back to recover from the shock of the concussion and tilted his helmet over his head.

A sudden blow struck the helmet which rolled a yard away. He reached for it with his free hand. The steel was dented at the back.

Oh, stop shelling, for Christ's sake! Give me peace. You've got me once, now leave me alone. I'll be all right if you just leave me alone.

He levered himself up on his right elbow and saw Martin lying grotesquely on his back, dead, eyes staring open, his shock of brown hair messed with blood and

15

sand. The cigarette still stuck between his bared, clenched teeth. Martin had it all right, and the girl back home wouldn't like to see him now, all messed up and twisted weirdly as if it hurt to be dead.

He remembered the blood spurting from his arm must be stopped. Was it the Doc who talked about using a stone to squeeze the artery? Good old Doc, he'd be having a busy time to-day.

He tucked a round stone, egg-size but flatter, under his armpit, and pressed the truncated limb with his other arm. The blood flow slowed down, and started again when he released the pressure. He squeezed again and held it. The stump was still trickling, but he was saving blood this way.

His mind struggled for articulation as he lay resting, for half an hour, an hour, two hours, he didn't know. You couldn't judge time in what looked a kind of hopeless business. The numbing arm was turning angrily to pain, not so bad as he thought it might be, yet devilish. Wouldn't be so bad if they stopped shelling.

If only I got back to the ditch for shelter—better chance of living there with mere blighty wounds*—no future lying here in these blasted explosions—but can't drag this silly forearm with me.

He struggled with his jack-knife held in the belt-loop of his shorts, and it was free. Shutting his teeth into the nail-slot, he drew open the blade. It took only a minute to cut the sinews of the shattered arm, and there wasn't much pain over the business.

He bit into his lower lip, gritted his teeth, and dragged himself half upright. The foot pained sharply, and he felt queer and dizzy.

Better wait a little longer until I've more strength.

He sank down again. The sky was a pale misty blue through the film of smoke haze and the sun was bright. It was peaceful up there above the air-burst shells in the

---

* wounds serious enough to have a man sent home as an invalid

16

great archivault of the heavens, and a lark was twittering near the centre of the battalion front, heedless of the earthly hell. A scurrying column of prisoners headed by a white flag was running the gauntlet of their own fire. The battalion were doing well then.

He began to think about Bill and the others in front, and then about the things he wouldn't be able to do single-handed, like knotting a tie and tying shoelaces, dressing up to go to the local dance at home. Perhaps you could do these things with practice. It would be fine when the war was over and you could gallivant again. Would a girl fall for a chap with one arm?

It was time for a cigarette. His matches would be in his left-hand trouser pocket. His right hand encircled his body, fumbling for the box. He held the box between his knees and lit up at first stroke.

A black ant darted into a little hollow a foot away from his nose. It peered over the edge and looked at him. He saw its mandibles quiver and its legs fidget nervously. Then it was still, as if making up its mind whether to come on and dare a detailed exploration.

He puffed a cloud of smoke straight at it. The ant ran quickly to the right in line with the top of his head, so that he had to raise his eyeballs to keep it in sight. He saw the knotty body start, and the black bulbous posterior rear up suddenly with a jerk of the mobile joints of its body. It looked so timid and scared. Perhaps it was going through the same emotions as he did while crouching on the start-line waiting to go over.

Once, back in the desert somewhere, one of his men had left the platoon's sugar ration on the ground with the bag open. A fine crowd of these little creatures they found there in the late afternoon, hundreds of them helping themselves gluttonously to the sugar, one stream rushing headlong to the booty and another stream poking with agitated fury among the white granules and scuttling back to the nest. It was like a constant two-way traffic

17

of black cars going between the metropolis and a seaside resort on a hot summer's day.

Ants liked sugar all right. There was sugar in blood. Some people suffered from diabetes. He didn't have diabetes, but he had sugar in his blood. Maybe the ant wanted the sugar. Well, he wasn't going to let the little bastard have any sugar, though God knows there was enough blood wetting the sand round him, and it wasn't going to be any use to him now.

The ant quivered again, and raced nearer him and past his head, down level with his abdomen, then stopped just as quickly beside a small, chipped grey stone. Slowly and cunningly he raised his right hand until it hovered over the unsuspecting ant. The hand slapped down. The ant struggled, tickling his palm. He plucked at it with two fingers, held it and a pinch of sand gently, held it, and squeezed it into a sticky mass between finger and thumb. A hot nausea flowed through him. He wiped his fingers on the grey stone and threw it away. Bad luck, ant, all that trouble for nothing.

He looked down at his arm, which lay detached at his side. It was white. He touched it with his right fore-finger. It was cold and firm, like touching smooth stone. The hairs, bleached golden by the sun of the long desert campaign, were slightly singed by the blast. The rigid fingers of the hand were bent a little. The thumb and forefinger were ink-stained. He wrote a letter to Helen yesterday and the pen leaked.

Sadly he looked at the watch still round his wrist. The hands—the ones that glowed so whitely in the darkness—had stopped at three minutes past six. The tiny second-hand was missing. The glass was smashed. The round black dial that he and Martin admired was dented.

Well, I guess Robbie got the best of the bargain after all.

R D Marshall

East is West

It was the first day he had been able to get around without his crutch and so the sergeant was rather pleased with himself. In fact, although it was still an hour to midday, he thought he deserved a beer. The Sudanese barman gave him a bottle of Stella and a glass and he hobbled back to the table where he had left his writing things. He put down the bottle and glass and then, supporting himself with his left hand on the chair, swung his left leg under the table. He lowered himself carefully on to the seat, with his weight on his good leg. The other one stuck out under the table and the heavy plaster rested on the iron bar that did duty for a heel.

It was still winter; so, though the sun outside was hot on the empty parade-ground, in here it was cool and there was no need to shut the windows or draw the blinds. As he looked out to the desert beyond the barrack huts he smiled. It wasn't so bad. This was one rest camp where they really did leave you alone. If only he didn't have this letter to write.

He poured the beer out slowly and watched the bubbles spring to the surface in a fine froth.

Two other chaps came in and began to play ping-pong in the far corner. Before long they had their shirts off and were playing only in their shorts. They still hadn't quite got rid of the yellow stage of jaundice.

The sergeant sipped his beer, then lit a cigarette and took a couple of draws, rather fast. A fly flicked at his mouth, thirsty, came back and flicked again. He brushed it away every time it came till it gave up and settled on his writing pad. It crawled till it found the place where the sweat of his hand had moistened the paper. Fingers spread so as not to give it the advantage of the draught, his hand smacked down. He brushed the squashed body aside and tore off that sheet. But there was another sheet beneath it, just as blank. He picked up his pen, suddenly.

'Dear Mrs Curtis,' he wrote. Then he put the pen down again. What the hell was he going to say? He'd written these letters before and it hadn't been easy. But this one seemed to be impossible altogether. What could he say? He could feel sorry for Curtis all right, poor sod. He was dead now, anyway, and it didn't matter much what sort of bloke he'd been. But that was no good. You couldn't very well say that to his mother. Was there anything in the whole rotten business you could say to her?

What did it have to happen for, anyway? Why should he have to write the bloody letter? It was only a bit of bad luck he'd come across Curtis at all.

Only it had looked like good luck then. Or it would have if he hadn't been so bomb-happy at the time that he took everything for granted. You took everything for granted at a time like that, when you'd just had your tank brew up under you and seen the only other bloke who managed to get out take a burst of Spandau in the chest and face before he even hit the ground.

He'd dragged George Black for a few yards until he saw there was no future in it. George was dead. The bullets were flying and the ammo in the tank would go up any minute. George slumped back when he let go. His shirt had ridden up the back and you could see where the bullets had come out.

Smoke, very dense and black, was pouring out of the tank. There was a terrific stink of oil and petrol and explosive. It wasn't the only tank either. You could see others of them going up in the same way all over the ridge.

He'd got his breath and his nerve back now. With-out looking at George he jumped to his feet and bolted into the smoke, going down wind with it. Anything to get away before she went up for good.

So it didn't seem surprising when he found himself being hauled into the cab of a Dodge pick-up. Or even when he saw it was Curtis and him with a captain's pips up, though the last time he'd seen him was in camp when they were Territorials and Curtis had only one stripe.

Curtis leaned across him and slammed the door to. The driver got back into gear and the truck went on, hell for leather.

'What happened, Sergeant? You all right?'

That brought him to a bit. Sergeant. It used to be Bob in the old days.

'OK, thanks. Tank went up. Only me and George got out. And they got George.'

He felt dopey and at the same time he wanted to talk. But he couldn't bring himself to call Curtis 'sir'. And he wasn't the sort of chap you could talk to about old George.

After a while he pulled himself together. 'Where are we off to?'

'B Ech HQ* at Brigade,' Curtis said.

As good as anywhere else. It'd been a good tank. You'd never get a pal like old George again.

But B Ech was pulling out when they got there. There was a fat major stamping round, giving all sorts of orders. A bit of a flap on.

'Get your truck into the convoy, Curtis,' said the major. 'There's a column of jerry armour coming along Trigh Capuzzo. We'll all be overrun and in the bag, if we don't get out of this a bit more smartly. Haven't you got that kit aboard yet, Rumbold?' He had turned towards a little fellow who was trying to shoulder a valise as big as himself into the back of a staff-car.

The sergeant couldn't see any sign of a Jerry column.

* B Echelon Headquarters

But he didn't care. It was their show now. They were officers. Let them handle it. None of his business. He'd had enough for just now.

'Come on, Grace, get a move on,' said Curtis.

The driver took the Dodge into the column. It was in desert formation but pretty ragged. The front vehicles began to move off without waiting. Those behind started off as best they could and began to find their places. The staff-car was the last to get away, the major even helping Rumbold with the camp-bed, he was in such a hurry. He cut across the Dodge's bows as he went up to the front. The sand behind him swirled in their open window.

'Put up that window, will you, Sergeant?' said Curtis.

'It looks as if we're going east,' said the sergeant.

'Where else? The show's a wash-out. You tankies have let him run all over you.'

The sergeant flushed. This from a man who wore the black beret,* even if he was in B Ech. But he said nothing.

Behind them, half left, on the ridge, they saw the flying sand of a column. Curtis opened the trap in the roof and looked through his glasses.

'Jerry,' he said, bending his knees and coming down. 'Put your foot on it, Grace.'

The driver went on at the same pace. He had to keep in formation.

A black gusher of smoke came up between two of the trucks in front. The convoy kept on. Another and another. One of the leading trucks, apparently unhit, began to blaze all the same. Men spilled over the tail-board on to the sand.

'Shall we pick some of them up, sir?' said Grace.

'No time. Let one of the three-tonners do it. They've got more room.'

But he felt the sergeant's stare. 'All right. Stop.'

'Only three of you. In the back. Hurry.'

*i.c. was himself a member of an armoured unit

22

Another truck, a fifteen hundred-weight, pulled up. A young lieutenant got out of the cab.

'Pile in with my blokes, the rest of you,' he said. 'Come on, you're not out blackberrying.' He watched them aboard, smiling. The sergeant began to feel better.

'They're all aboard, Grace,' Curtis said. 'What are you waiting for? They're bound to get us if we hang round any longer.'

As they moved off there was a crash behind them.

The sergeant looked back. At first there was nothing but smoke. When it cleared he saw the other truck coming on. The officer was standing with his head and shoulders halfway out of the trap, his binoculars resting on the roof of the cab in front. He waved. The sergeant waved back. A good bloke.

The convoy had become a single column now with wide intervals between trucks. You could feel all they had in common was that they wanted to go fast and in the same direction.

B Ech bastards, the sergeant thought. He was already homesick for his squadron. What had happened to them all? Were things really as bad as this?

'Step on it, Grace.'

'Yes, sir,' said the driver. He drove at the same steady pace. He's all right, that chap, the sergeant thought.

'Any idea where we are?' he asked.

'El Gubbi is on the right somewhere,' said Curtis. 'We should get to the wire soon.'

The way he said it it didn't sound as if he had much idea. They seemed to be going south-east now. So they'd probably strike the wire all right. Anyhow, it was Curtis' business. He was the officer. And didn't he know it? But he was the officer all the same. You couldn't get past that. But the sergeant couldn't help remembering they used to call him Blanco in the Terries.

Curtis took out a packet of Players. The sergeant hadn't had a smoke since the battle began that morning.

But he was damned if he was going to ask for one. He looked straight ahead through the windscreen. The sand from the truck in front uncoiled and expanded towards them, like a spring. Curtis was tapping a cigarette against the packet.

'Have one?'

'Thanks,' said the sergeant and took it. There were tears of relief in his eyes. The driver's face looked very set.

'What about the driver?' the sergeant said.

'Have one, Grace?' said Curtis, quite amiably.

'Thanks very much, sir,' said the driver.

It was getting on towards four when they came to the gap in the wire. There were no MPs* there. Trucks had converged on it from all directions. You could see from all the different unit signs mixed up together, odds and sods of all sorts, that there'd been a pretty fair MFU,† a real balls-up. Even if everyone hadn't been going the wrong way.

'We'll be hours getting through at this rate,' said Curtis.

The sergeant got out of the truck.

'I'll have one too,' Curtis said. He got out and began to unbutton his fly. But the sergeant was walking towards the gap.

'Where are you off to?' called Curtis.

'Must try and help straighten this out,' said the sergeant.

All it needed was someone to see that too many didn't try to get through at once. Soon he had the traffic going in a steady stream. Luckily no Jerry planes had turned up in time.

The Dodge came up. 'No point in staying there all night,' Curtis said. 'You might as well jump aboard. Let some other mug take a turn.'

*Military policemen
†Major foul-up

24

On the other side the trucks had streamed away as fast as they got through. No one had any notion where the leading truck had got to. The convoy was well scattered, disorganized.

After a while the sergeant saw they might as well give up trying to keep in convoy. 'Let's pull out and have something to eat,' he said. 'If you've got any grub, that is.'

'There's plenty in the back,' Curtis said. 'But do you think it's all right? He might be pretty close behind us.' He seemed rather subdued.

'Might as well take a chance. We can always bolt for it.'

They got out and went round to the back of the truck. Curtis undid the flap. The three men who'd got aboard and his batman were sitting there, with knees drawn up. Their faces were caked with the fine sand that had got through the flap. They climbed out stiffly. One of them was a corporal.

The batman got some biscuits and bully* and a tin of cheese. 'Here you are, sir.' Curtis took some.

'Have some, Sergeant?' said the batman.

'Thanks, chum.'

'There you are now, Corp.' The batman passed what was left to the corporal and he began to share it out.

'Think I should brew up and make a cup of char, sir?' said the batman.

'Christ, no. No time.'

The others all looked glum.

'What's the next move?' said the sergeant.

'There's nothing to stop the Jerries between here and Mersa. We'll have to go south-east a good bit before we turn up to join the reserves there.'

'Nothing between us and Mersa?' said the sergeant.

'I know what I'm talking about.'

The sergeant shrugged. Perhaps he did know. His own

*corned beef

25

unit had been fighting off and on for three days. He had no idea what had been happening anywhere beyond what you could see from the tank. And not much about that either. But if Curtis was right things were pretty bad.

'Planes,' said one of the men.

There were three of them, coming out of the sun.

The sergeant had noticed a Bren in the back of the truck. He grabbed it and fitted a magazine.

'Put her on my shoulder,' said the corporal, running round to his front.

'OK, Corp.' He rested the barrel on the corporal's shoulder and waited.

'What's your unit?' he asked.

'I was orderly room corporal at B Ech HQ.'

'Good for you.' He wasn't sure what he meant. But he liked the corporal.

'Just as well the traffic's mostly through the gap,' the corporal said. 'What a target it was.'

The planes curved away and down towards a column of transport that had followed them through the gap and was now dispersed on the ridge opposite. They peeled off and dived, machine-gunning and bombing. There was some scattered AA* fire.

When the planes had dropped their stuff and wheeled off west again, the sergeant and the corporal walked back to the truck.

'That sounded like Jerry AA to me,' said the sergeant.

'Rubbish, Sergeant,' Curtis said. He got up and brushed the sand from his battledress. 'It can't be. They can't have got here already.'

'The planes did look a bit like Tomahawks,' said the corporal.

'Nonsense.' Contradicting them made Curtis feel more confident. 'We'll drive over and see what the news is.'

This time the sergeant kept a look out from the trap.

* anti-aircraft

26

'Could I borrow your glasses?' he called down.

Curtis got them out of their case. But already the truck was close enough.

'Jerries,' the sergeant said as he shot down through the trap. 'Quick, driver, left hand down.' They were no more than a couple of hundred yards away.

'We'll have to turn it in,' Curtis said.

The sergeant stared at him. His mouth was slightly open, face pale. He did not meet the sergeant's eye.

'Flat out,' said the sergeant across Curtis to the driver. There was a slight flush on the driver's cheekbone and a little ridge of cartilage riding up and down where the jaws joined. The truck righted itself as it came out of the swerve, the driver's foot hard on the accelerator.

They were running across the enemy's front now, a good target. The sergeant could see Jerries at the turrets of a few tanks which had been hidden behind the ridge. Resting up or getting ready to laager* for the night.

A rip of bullets smashed through glass.

'It's no go,' said Curtis. 'We'd better turn it in.'

The bullets had smashed diagonally through the right-hand window, above the driver's head. The sergeant stared through the windscreen to the front, watching the desert come flying to meet them and waiting for the finishing burst. If he were driving he would hardly have had the spare energy to feel like this. He did not want to look at Curtis.

He got up and peered over the edge of the trap, looking back. The enemy trucks were well behind, perhaps already out of effective range. He came down into the cab again.

'I knew we shouldn't have stopped there,' Curtis said.

They drove on and didn't stop till it was safe to take a bearing.

'Don't you think we should head up towards the coast?' the sergeant said.

*form a temporary camp

'They're probably all along the coast road by now,' Curtis said. 'They'll have come down Halfaya Pass, I'll bet.'

He had the compass and the sergeant was too tired to argue. But he suspected the navigation was very much by guess and by God. It would have been more comfortable if they'd had the coast road to guide them.

Last light came.

'I think it's safe to turn more to the north now,' Curtis said.

'Or perhaps brew up and bed down for the night?' suggested the sergeant. There didn't seem much sense in just plunging on through the night. And it was risky, too.

'We must try and join up with the rest at Mersa as soon as we can.'

But he told the driver to stop all the same and they had some more bully and biscuits. The men were getting a bit jittery. They'd obviously got Curtis pretty well summed up already. They sat off in a group by themselves in the sand and talked in low voices. The driver was evidently telling them how close they'd been to the bag. The batman skipped about, putting things away. The sergeant was left with Curtis. Curtis didn't talk much. He had become more and more the officer as he felt his prestige going down.

'Come on, men,' he said at last. 'No time to waste. All aboard.'

The sergeant drove for a while. Then Curtis took over. The driver was supposed to be having a sleep. But it was his truck and, though both Curtis and the sergeant drove well, he was uneasy till it was his turn again. The sergeant dozed, waking at heavier jolts, then going off again. Once he was back in his tank just after it caught fire. Only this time the hatch had jammed. After that he didn't sleep for quite a while and even managed to ask Curtis for a cigarette. When it was finished he slept again.

28

A shell had smashed the tank track. Yet it seemed to be going on clanking.

'Sounds like a bit of wire or something caught in the mudguard,' he woke to hear the driver saying. 'We'd better stop and have a look.'

They got out and had a look. The truck had hit a single strand of wire and dragged it along.

'A minefield,' said the sergeant.

'It can't be,' Curtis said. 'They've never got as far as this.'

'It might be one of ours. We'd be wiser to stop where we are till first light. There's not even a moon.'

'Look,' said the driver. 'Flares.'

They turned round. Back the way they had come the flares were shooting up into the sky, lingering, then dropping slowly to a darkness that closed on them before they reached the ground.

'Jerries,' said Curtis.

'Might be our chaps.'

'I tell you, Sergeant, there's nothing to stop them between where they are and Mersa. We've got to get on.'

'I think we should stop where we are till first light. We'll be able to see then whether we're in a minefield or not.'

'And get picked up by the Jerries in the morning just for fear of a few imaginary mines? I thought you had more guts than that, Sergeant.' This was his revenge for the afternoon.

'I still think it's crazy.'

'It doesn't matter what you think. I'm the superior officer here and I say we're going on.' There had been a fresh outbreak of flares.

The driver had unwound the wire from the axle. They went back to the cab.

'I'll tell you what,' Curtis said, amiable again. 'You take a spell at the wheel and I'll get out on the mudguard, just to please you.'

29

The sergeant took her along slowly. The driver sat beside him, very uneasy, and then after a bit climbed out on the left. The sergeant's eyes strained out through the windscreen to the moving glimmer of desert in front. He thought how thin the flooring was that separated him from the upward blast that might come at any moment.

When it came it flung him through the door and out on his face. The flash left his eyes and he was staring at the sand, his ears singing on this side of a wall of deafness. He got up still stupid, and staggered out of the black fumes. He found himself at the back of the truck.

'Mines,' he said to the faces that stared out at him.

Then he remembered Curtis and the driver. He came round to the front again. Curtis seemed to be trying to raise himself on his hands and each time falling on his face, half-sideways. The driver was coming round the bonnet from the other side. He seemed all right.

Curtis was lying on his face when they got to him, no longer trying to get up. The sergeant turned him on his back. His right leg was gone, from the thigh. The left foot was hanging from the shinbone by a few ragged strands.

'Get out your field-dressings,' the sergeant said to the others who had all come up. He got out his own as well.

Curtis was beginning to struggle again. 'Sit on him,' said the sergeant to the driver. 'He mustn't see his legs.'

The driver sat on Curtis and lit him a cigarette. The corporal knelt and kept his finger pressed down on the artery just below where it joined the groin. The sergeant from the other side tried to find enough thigh to get a purchase for the tourniquet. Curtis had begun to scream now and heaved from time to time. Each time the blood gulped out more swiftly than ever. The dressings were soaking already. The sergeant did his best with the tourniquet and then turned to the left leg. The ragged trouser was in the way.

30

'Anyone got a knife?'

Nobody had, but the sergeant remembered seeing one in the cab. Quicker to find it himself. His own foot was giving trouble now but he got to the cab, fumbled for the jack-knife which had slipped down behind the seat, got it and came back. He got on a second tourniquet and dressings.

Suddenly the corporal flopped. He had fainted. Curtis gave a sort of final heave and sat up. He saw what had happened to his legs.

'My legs,' he said, 'Jesus Christ, my legs.'

The blood was still coming from the right thigh, in spite of the tourniquet. Curtis got weaker and his voice quieter. 'Why did it have to be me?' he kept moaning. 'Oh, sweet Jesus Christ, why did it have to be me?'

The corporal came to and tried to stop the bleeding with his fingers on the artery again.

'Shall I make a cup of char on the primus, Sergeant?' said the batman.

'OK. Here, corporal, give us a strain on this, will you?'

But it was no good. The blood kept getting away, soaking the dressings, the sand. And the pain was getting worse as the shock passed off. Curtis seemed to be going out of his mind with it. Sometimes he cried like a baby and called out for his mother.

Then he seemed to get himself under control again. He recognized the sergeant.

'Bob,' he said, 'shoot me, Bob, for Christ's sake. I can't stand it. Shoot me.'

The sergeant crouched beside him.

He did not know whether it was a long time or a short time before Curtis died.

He had to cut away the boot from his own foot then. Its aching did not let him sleep and he kept hearing Curtis and seeing Curtis, though Curtis was silent now under his last blanket. He was glad when first light came.

31

The corporal and he stabbed about with bayonets till they found a spot where there were no mines. They dug a grave and buried Curtis. His body was the colour of skimmed milk.

The batman made tea and they had breakfast, bully and biscuit. The driver stood with his mug in his hand, looking at the wrecked wheel and mudguard and shaking his head. The sergeant's foot was too swollen now for him to walk.

When the column of Indians who had leaguered* a mile away that night rescued them from the minefield the sergeant had to be carried.

If it had been poor old George that had asked me I'd have done it for him, the sergeant was thinking now. I'd have known it was all right if it'd been a pal like George.

He hobbled up to the bar to get another beer. 'Dear Mrs Curtis,' was as far as he'd got. It was as far as he'd got yesterday, and the day before.

Dan Davin

*Camped

Zero at Rabaul

We met the sun half-way that morning, on the leg from Seven Mile to Hood Point, before we turned north-east to cross the Owen Stanleys.* We were climbing to gain height for the crossing, our aircraft very heavy and sloppy with its extra petrol load and, as we gained the height of the parallel line of near blue mountains, the sun shot above the darker outline of the distant range. It was day; and I looked at it with mistrust.

I was not at all happy about the job we were on and I knew my second pilot felt the same way. Harry had been unusually quiet that morning as we ate our warm beans and drank hot tea from scalding pannikins; and that was unlike Harry. I didn't like Harry to be quiet.

We were to do a daylight recco of Kavieng and Rabaul. We were to return if there was no cloud cover. That was all very well on paper, written out in Ops Room in Gordon's neat hand: return if no cloud cover. But in the first place, when you are as inexperienced as I was then, you do not like returning empty-handed to the Cat. boys † waiting for your information before taking off.

Then again, in spite of a bad weather report—fine and cloudless, visibility twenty miles—supposing there were cloud cover over the target. I could only expect it to be scattered at that time of the day, and over the land. That left a clear sea crossing from New Ireland to Rabaul with both Jap fighter nests well stirred up. I had sampled the Kavieng fighters several nights before when Dick dived his Cat. into cloud with three of them spitting fire on his tail; a cloud which, my navigation told me, contained a

* a range of mountains in south-east New Guinea
† Cat. = Catalina, an aircraft used for sea reconnaissance

33

four-thousand-foot peak. I waited for the bump or the shells to burst, and when neither came, I agreed with Dick that I would take the chance of the bump in preference any time.

It was the sea crossing now that had me worried, for I reasoned this way: If we went to Kavieng first and made our get-away through cloud down New Ireland, we would then have to cross in the open to Rabaul, whose fighters no doubt would be expecting us. And it was unpleasant to be expected in the open in those days. So my plan was this: To visit Rabaul first and then turn due west for fifty miles as if returning home. This would be over the land and I could expect some cloud support. Fifty miles west I intended to turn north-east, run over Kavieng, lose height through cloud to tree-top height and make my get-away due west low over the water. When out of danger I intended to set course for Salamaua.

That was my plan; I had thought it out during an air raid the night before while Jap bombers circled unmolested above the moonlit cirrus. And I went over it again now as we climbed towards the range.

The sun seemed to climb faster than we did. Its light slanted down into the undulating lowlands beneath us so that the ridges separated themselves sharply from the darkness of the valleys and stood defined like the ribs of some gigantic fossil. Wisps of low cloud added to this effect. It was as if some cotton wool tufts had remained stuck to the bones after their unpacking. Jungle covered the ribs and knotted backbone like moss. This country had been dead a long time.

We crossed the main range at ten thousand feet. Clouds were already coming up to meet us, clambering from the peaks like apes into the higher air. This was a good sign but meant that they would be above fifteen thousand for our return. Over Buna the clouds broke, leaving only blueness before us; blue sea and blue air.

A coral reef scarred the sea under our starboard wing, looking for the moment like the wake of a ship. In the distance a Gothic cumulus like a crazy scarecrow sat on air. We checked our guns, lined up the I.C.,* Harry gave the camera a final check. We felt better now that we were on the way.

I remembered Bob. He had taken off on a job somewhat like this about a week before. I drove up from the town over the dusty road with his operation order. He read through it but he seemed all the time to be thinking of something else. He waved his hand and took off. I have always liked watching a Hudson take off. Until its wheels are up it seems to be pulled off the ground by sheer brute force. You can hear the horses straining. Then the wheels tuck themselves up in three slow jerks and the aircraft begins to fly. A Hudson looks very good with its wheels up as it skims the trees at the beginning of its climb. But I watched that day with a different emotion. Bob would not come back. I was convinced of it. And standing there on the tender roof watching the dust settle and Bob turning on to course, I think I felt more emotion than he did. I know I felt more disturbed then than when I was ordered out on this job. We were talking over a bottle of warm beer of what we would do on leave in Sydney when Pedro came up and in his slow way told me I was to go out next morning. I felt fear immediately. But you do not write yourself off in your own mind with the finality with which I wrote off Bob from the top of the truck that day. Your mind always brings you home, damaged perhaps, but alive, from its most daring fantasies. As well as this, you have other things that must be thought over. When I dismissed Bob, I had time to pause, to allow the luxury of sadness to shape itself. Confronted with the same risk myself, there was my plan to think out, my aircraft to be teed up, so that my immediate fear was pushed to the back of my mind and

*intercom

35

became a vague apprehension which sharpened all actions. This apprehension sits buried in the mind, ready to flare into sudden fear when an enemy convoy is sighted or fighters appear. It acts as a spur and a warning to caution. It is like the sign at a railway crossing: 'Danger. Beware of trains.'

I called up Harry on the I.C.

'Do you see anything there, dead ahead?'

'Where? Fighters?'

'Cloud.'

'Whacko.'

Cloud lay over the highlands of New Britain, massed cloud, yellow with distance. Like robbers who see an open church door, we headed for it.

We made landfall at Gasmata. The runways were deserted, pockmarked with bomb craters. I remembered that the Wirraway boys had landed there on their way to Rabaul. Two of them, slowed up by the long grass, had hit their tail wheels in the water taking off. The grass had been mown since then and the Wirraway boys had been shot down in seven minutes over Rabaul.

It was not far from Gasmata to the highlands over which the cloud crawled. I had marked the same route on the maps of the Wirraway pilots and they had been warned that they were to take the coastal route if the day were cloudy. Cloud had taken on a different meaning since then. It was no longer to be avoided. Its down draughts, its ice, and its magnetic storms were forgotten when fighters were about. We wrapped its greyness around us and felt secure. The wing-tips became our farthest horizon.

Harry came up with chocolate. We munched and watched the water stream from our wings. It trickled into my boots. I felt happy.

'How long to go?'

'Should be there in thirty-six minutes,' Harry said.

'Thirty-six?'

36

'And a half,' said Harry. And he joined his thumb and forefinger as if throwing a dart.

Ten minutes before E.T.A.* I checked the fuel. The auxiliary tank was almost empty, leaving the main tanks full. I changed to left front and once more checked all instruments. The aircraft with its reduced load handled better now. The clouds were still thick but they broke occasionally, revealing patches of rainsoaked jungle ten thousand feet below. The next break revealed the coast south of Wotom Island. We were almost there. For a moment I mistook a small island for an aircraft carrier and we circled. Then we swung back onto course for Rabaul.

As we broke cover the harbour lay several miles ahead and below us. The cloud formed a crescent to the south and to the east, leaving the harbour clear except for scattered high, fair-weather cumulus. In the distance I could see the blue outline of New Ireland.

We made our camera run directly over Rabaul township, turned at the Beehives and swung around over Lakunai. There were about thirty ships in the harbour. Three destroyers lay in a triangle where I had seen them two days previously. There were a further three destroyers in harbour and the merchant-men were dispersed at anchor in approximately two scattered lines. Further construction work had been done on the building area at the lower drome. There were small grey and brown aircraft lined along both sides of the runways and the flying boats lay with their noses into wind outside the mouth of the river. The only movement I could see was that of a crazy little tug which circled and twisted in the harbour mouth. Not an A/A burst was fired.

I counted the number of ships, noting their disposition and types on a small map I had of the harbour. I counted the number of flying boats. But all the time another part of my mind was noting other things. It noted the sunlight

* estimated time of arrival

37

on the harbour, the dots of the coconut trees, the slow smoke rising from the brown-fissured mouth of Matupi. That part of my mind would not be convinced that there was a war on this soft spring morning. As far as it was concerned I was not five hundred miles from home over enemy territory. And I found myself ready to laugh at the crazy panic of that little tug.

Then I saw the Zero.* It was taking off from Lakunai, a small silver T pulling up over the tops of the coconut palms. I thought quickly. I had not quite finished the recco and I had at the most four minutes before the Zero gained our height. I warned the crew and put the aircraft into a steep turn over the harbour making my final notes.

Three minutes had elapsed since the Zero took off and I was just straightening from the turn, headed for cloud, when I felt a sudden hammer blow on my left wrist and pins and needles in my hand. At the same moment the instrument panel began to fall to pieces. I looked at my wrist in surprise. Where my watch had been there was a round blue hole. The palm of my hand was ripped open and the end of my little finger was missing. The bullet had evidently come from behind, penetrated my wrist, passed through the control wheel—there was an inch gap in its circumference—and taken off my little finger before lodging in the airspeed indicator.

And I was surprised; completely surprised. I am convinced that a man, until he sees bullets flying around him, does not basically realize that war is serious, that the enemy is out to kill him. Height detaches the bomber pilot from actual violence. He runs over a ship; four small darts slide from the belly of his aircraft and disappear below. Looking down he sees a plume of smoke start from the stricken ship and he congratulates himself on his good bombing. He knows little of the panic and destruction where his small darts have struck. He has lived a normal peaceful life and he is immune from this until his instru-

*a Japanese aircraft

38

ment panel begins to fall apart and he sees his hand flapping suddenly like a dying fish.

I looked at the waving of my hand with surprise and a certain nausea. Then I glanced around into the aircraft cabin. It was filled with smoke. This, I thought, is the end. And again I was filled with a strange surprise; surprise that I, having done and thought the things that make up my particular existence, should end my life here in a burning aircraft ten thousand feet above a town I had lived in not a month back. For I felt no doubt that this was the end. It was a visible fact. It took this to convince the subtleties of my imagination that I was as vulnerable as Bob.

During the second that this thought filled my mind, my hand had jammed the throttles through the gate, loosened the catch of the emergency exit and the aircraft was diving for cloud while my feet jumped alternately on left and right rudder. I heard the turret guns open up again and in my mind I saw the silver fighter diving in for its second attack. Ken Erwin had given me an image of a Zero attacking. He was attacked head on. Vapour flags streamed from either wing-tip and smoke from the forward guns. I saw this image now. Glass fell once more from the instrument panel and then grey cloud immersed us; we were soaked in cloud.

No flames belched from the cabin so with the vision of that silver fighter still on our tail, I kept the aircraft in its dive, turning steeply one way, straightening up and turning the other. I thought of mountains, but they did not worry me. We had been in cloud at least a minute before I realized that I was flying without instruments. I cleaned the compass of a film of silver dust and found we were once more headed for Rabaul. I cleaned the artificial horizon and, levelling out, turned due west following my original plan. The airspeed indicator and both altimeters were shot away. Several other instruments were missing, but the petrol, air temperature and one cylinder head temperature gauge were undamaged as were the rev and boost counters. I noted that the smoke was not increasing but still hung in the air like silver dust. Then I saw Harry.

Harry had been busy with the camera when he noticed a large portion of the tail unit disappear. At the same time he felt a concussion in his body. Looking at the camera he thanked God that it had not been hit. He struggled into his parachute harness and not until he had walked up to the W/T* cabin, where he suddenly sat down, did he realize how badly he was wounded. His right index finger was shot away and his second finger hung down his palm from a thin cord. His left arm was paralysed from a bullet lodged in his biceps, and blood flowed from a large hole in the calf of one leg. He sat there unable to move while smoke curled around him. Looking at his damaged hand he wondered how the devil he had managed to clip on his parachute harness.

It was there that Jock found him. Jock was in the bomb aimer's position taking notes when bullets began to whistle above his head and he saw them spraying out past the nose. We discovered later that there were two hundred and sixty odd holes in the aircraft from the two attacks. Jock climbed the companionway and, seeing Harry, he turned and was sick down the companionway. When I saw Harry I felt no emotion whatsoever. I was hit; I thought the aircraft was on fire; in half-a-minute it had been turned from an orderly unit into a butcher's shop. I thought and felt certain things for a few over-whelming seconds. And then my emotions ceased to function. Like so many good coal miners, they went on strike. I looked at Harry and told myself that it was only to be expected. Jock, however, knowing little of what had happened, was taken by surprise. His system rebelled against the evidence of his eyes and he was sick.

Immediately afterwards he got to work. He cleaned

* wireless telegraphy

up the sea-marker that had been hit and was filling the aircraft with aluminium dust. He put out some smoulder- ing ammunition. He came forward to fix me up. A tourniquet made from wireless leads proved too painful for my arm so he wrapped it up in a shirt and left it at that. He told me that our rear gunner had got it on both legs and he went back to fix him up.

I am not sure whether the rear gunner lost sight of the Zero during my steep turn or whether he was follow- ing the inexperienced instructions I had given him earlier that he was to pick up as much information as possible while we were over the target. Nor am I sure whether the Zero that attacked us was the one I saw taking off or whether another had dived from high cloud cover while we were watching the former. At all events the attacker was already pressing home his attack when our gunner saw him. He warned me then but the I.C. had already been hit. He got in a good burst as the Zero pulled away, showing his belly, and although wounded, fought it out during the next attack. He estimated that the Zero must have received fairly extensive damage. He did not leave the turret until we were well out of danger in the cloud. A concentrated burst of explosive cannon had ripped a large hole in the turret just between his open knees.

We came into the clear about thirty miles west of Rabaul. I judged that we were about two thousand feet above the jungle. There were storm clouds to the south-east so I turned into them for home. It was then that Harry surprised me. Sitting in his blood he asked if we were going on to Kavieng. Going on to Kavieng! This thought had not even entered my head. I was going home. Directly I saw my hand flapping, out of control, to get home or as near home as possible, had become instinctive. And now Harry asked me if we were going on. Then I understood him. Harry had not expected to return from this job. And I realized that, at the back of

41

my mind, I hadn't either. I grinned at Harry and he grinned back and we seemed to say to one another: 'Well, we've been shot up but we're going home. Things weren't so bad after all.'

But could we make it? In the clear I had taken stock of the damage. The engines were going well but there were several bullet holes through the cowlings. And all the tanks were leaking. I was shocked to find that one tank was using more fuel than the one I was running on. Next, could I make it myself? I felt the blood from my arm dribbling from its shirt wrapping into my boots as the rain had, happily, an hour previously. Fear kept me from looking at my wound again. I wanted to keep it shut away from myself.

I tried to reason with my instinct to head for Moresby. Salamaua was closer. And there was no fifteen thousand feet crossing. But there was no doctor as far as I knew at Salamaua, only a small detachment of New Guinea Riflemen; communication between Salamaua and Moresby had been out of order that morning before we left; it was unlikely that an aircraft would be able to get over there that day. I told myself this but I knew that I would head for Moresby, anyway. If the fuel was low before the range crossing, I would divert to Salamaua.

So our return became a race for time against the leaking fuel. I could no longer nurse the motors. Here was another excuse. With the throttles open to the gate, I eased up the nose and began to climb in the general direction of Port Moresby. By this time we had already gained some height and the boost was little more than twenty-eight inches.

I tried out George.* Although the directional gyro was damaged, the bank and climb held. I looked around the cockpit. Everything was covered with a thin layer of silver, instruments, controls, and even Jock's face as he lit a cigarette and put it in my mouth. My small map of

*the automatic pilot

Rabaul had been shot out of my hand, and this with the maps of the whole area was covered in blood and silver dust.

I drew on the cigarette and began to cipher a message to base. Half-way through Harry called to me that the engines were losing power. The manifold pressures were falling rapidly. So we were for it after all. It would have been better to finish at Rabaul than crash-land here through cloud in the central New Britain jungle. But it might be ice. Rime was frosting the windscreen and wings. I put in the carburettor heats. The roar of the engines opened out again; the manifold pressures built up. Time once more moved forward. Jock was going over the wireless. He came forward and told me it had been damaged. I put aside the recco report and sat back looking into the greyness. As we gained height things seemed to matter less and less. My arm lost all feeling and lay numb and still on my knee. And as the ache receded, so the meaning began to slip away from this race against fuel.

We came out of cloud high over the jungle to the northward of Gasmata. The sea was bright with sun and the outline of the coast disappeared westward in blue haze. I found myself saying: 'Don't let there be any fighters.' It would be necessary then to swing the aircraft around, dive for the yellow cloud over the highlands, creep west through cloud with the fuel gauges falling. Here, with the aircraft climbing, I could sit back in the sun where nothing very much seemed to matter. I began to think of home.

I had been thinking of home only the night before and now, no doubt, I would be sent home. My wife and I would take a flat at King's Cross,* a flat high up overlooking the harbour. We would stay in bed late and when we got up we would wander around the shops in the sun buying fruit and salads and cold meats. We would take

*a suburb of Sydney

43

them back to the flat and there would be cold beer on the ice and the day would be both cool and warm so that we needn't wear a great deal. And the curtains would blow in occasionally in the wind from the harbour.

I pulled myself together with a start and slapped myself several times hard on the side of the face. I checked the gauges and the course. I could see the cloud now over the Owen Stanleys and I knew I had been wise to keep her climbing. It was towering above the range in great sunlit ramparts. There were eighty gallons in the right rear tank as we crossed the coast on course north of Buna. Salamaua lay to the right in a sun haze.

Climbing still, we had to divert slightly to the south to avoid the tops of the cumulus. I judged that we were at about eighteen thousand feet; the temperature gauge read below zero, but I was taking no chances now of hitting the hills. Beyond the cumulus tops lay a wide cloud layer whose brilliant whiteness hurt the eyes. There were occasional breaks.

Harry said: 'We must be about there.' He had not moved from his position on the floor and his hand looked grotesque.

I throttled back and nosed the aircraft down through a wispy cloud break. And there below, ringed in storm, lay Port Moresby. I checked the gauges before diving. There were forty gallons; petrol to spare.

Diving, I hoped the tail unit would hold. We spiralled, passing through scattered rain and wispy cloud. And all the time below lay Moresby, the hillsides baked brown and grey by sun; its inlets and islands defined as on a map; the sea glassy, coloured by strips of green shallows; but ruffled and wind-lined to the north-west by a sudden squall. We got into the rain from the squall and I pulled out fifty feet from the water over the light in the harbour mouth. In the clear we headed for Seven Mile. I checked the tank and we had five gallons of fuel left in one tank. All the others read empty. The change of pressure in the dive must have opened the holes in the tank and let the petrol out. I had two alternatives: To land the aircraft on the water in the harbour or to try to make Seven Mile. We headed for Seven Mile. If we didn't make it, it still did not matter a great deal. On the water there was every chance of Harry and our gunner drowning, if not all of us.

We sneaked over the coastal hills and there in the valley between its rough skirting ranges was Seven Mile. Jock was beside me. I put down the under-carriage and it clicked home. We checked the wheels visually. They looked all right. The trim I found had been shot away. We turned in for the approach. I had not had time or fuel to check the flaps higher up so I decided to put them down and if the aircraft swung, to bring them straight up again.

'Right, flaps,' I called to Jock.

Jock pressed down the flap lever and at the same moment my port engine coughed and spluttered. The aircraft swung heavily to port. The starboard engine coughed.

It then became necessary to do a number of things. It really did not matter. We would land on our guts in the scrub-covered gully but these things had to be done first.

'Up with flaps.'

I shoved the nose forward keeping the speed at what I judged to be ninety knots. I took the stick in my left hand and power seemed to come back to it. With my right, I changed to another tank, for there might be a few gallons left, and pumped hard on the wobble pump. The engines coughed, picked up. Still priming, we cleared a pile of petrol drums and the wheels touched on the runway. As the aircraft ran down the gravelled strip, she seemed to limp and there was a thudding sound of rubber.

'The starboard tyre's gone.'

'All right.' It did not matter any more. I got my left arm over the stick, holding it back and the left aileron down. With my right hand I pulled on the brake, counteracting swing with full left rudder. The tail kicked, came down and the aircraft slowed up. Slowly it turned and stopped at right angles to the runway.

'Right, cut.'

The engines cut and there was stillness.

Now out, out of this aircraft, get your feet on ground. I stumbled through the silver-coated cabin, out of the door into the sunlight.

I began walking rapidly towards the huts which stood amongst slender gum trees on the other side of the runway. A tender swung through dust from the hut road making for the aircraft. I waved it on. My feet had taken control of me and it was as if they were off to catch a train. They would not stop. I did not realize what a spectacle I must have looked, carrying my hand still wrapped in a shirt, my face and hands and knees coloured silver as if badly burnt. Pedro leapt from the side of the tender. A car drew up and he pushed me in. My tongue immediately took over from my legs. I was still talking rapidly when we pulled up outside the main hut.

There I made my report to Col. It was a relief to be able to talk without interruption. My tongue ran forward detailing the ships in the harbour, the construction work on the lower drome while Col scribbled notes on a pad, trying to keep up. Men stood around, their fingers still marking the places in their magazines where they had been reading. Pedro offered me brandy but I refused. That, I told myself, would be the end. If only I can keep on talking. If I keep talking I won't break down.

An hour later, in hospital, I was happier than I have ever been. I was washed and clean, ready for the operation. My arm was not painful and I felt slightly drunk at still being alive. And I was going home. The army nurses seemed unbelievably beautiful.

David Campbell

46

All in the Day

Whenever people are arguing about who won the war, my thoughts, for some reason, go to a man who was known to me as Taylor 08. Not that he was doing much about the war at the time when I knew him—that happened later, when he was in Italy and I in Baghdad.

I became aware of his separate existence on a route march, when 'B' Company was ascending a steep hill east of Marlow. (In the autumn of 1940, having new men to toughen quickly, we were doing longish marches in Field Service Order every Tuesday and Friday.) The first thing I noticed was a steel helmet of which the crown came level with the shoulders of the man in front. Beneath this helmet, when I stooped a little, I saw the thin and pasty face of a boy who looked about nineteen. He was bathed in sweat; and he was smiling to himself, with his teeth together, as men do when in pain.

I marched beside him for a little way.

'Are you all right?' I asked.

'O.K., thanky' sir!'

He didn't look it. At every pace his diminutive legs had to travel about nine inches further than nature intended, and I guessed from my own experience that the heavy ammunition boots were a torture to him: he was, I discovered, a gas-fitter's mate, just three weeks in uniform.

'You can stick it out, anyway?'

'Cor, easy sir!' He wriggled his rifle loose from one shoulder and slung it on the other, heaved at his equipment and spat out the pip of an imaginary orange. 'Nice walk in the country and the Army pays yer—money for jam, sir!'

But the state of his feet, when I saw them after the

47

march, was gruesome. I told him to report sick and get them some attention.

Shortly before one o'clock, next day, Brewer the C.S.M.* came to me in the office tent with the familiar expression of one who is being put-upon.

'Taylor 08 asking for interview. I've told him the time for interviews is after Company Office. These young recruits, you know, sir—'

On this question, however, I always took a line of my own. I said firmly, 'I'll see him!'

The Taylor who was indignantly marched in to me was a different man from the one of the day before. The impudent swagger, the guts, had gone. This was a homesick child.

'How are the feet?' I asked him.

He didn't seem to hear me. Without speaking, he laid on my table a telegram.

I scarcely needed to read it: in those September days every morning brought half a dozen telegrams which were always much the same. '*Bombed out last night*', this one said. '*Please come immediate love Liz.*'

I said, 'I'm sorry about this, I'm most terribly sorry!' and I went on with a piece which I had almost got by heart: he mustn't worry too much, the authorities had everything under control, they would find somewhere for his wife to live.

He waited till I came to the end, and then he said, 'I got to go, sir! I can borrow the fare. Be on parade termorrer, sir—I only want 'alf a day.'

This was Brewer's cue. His face already looked as if it had been pickled in cement. His voice came on like a jerky record on the gramophone:

'Can't be done, sir! Command Order, sir—London area out of bounds to all personnel not on duty.'

I said to Taylor, 'I'm afraid that's true. It's a very definite order.'

* Company Sergeant-Major

48

To the haggard child before me this made no sense at all. He looked at me as if I were a dog refusing to perform some simple trick out of sheer stupidity.

'See how it is, sir, the wife, sir, she's got no head on her for business an' all. Three kids, we've got, sir.'

I explained again, as patiently as I was able: the order had been made for the general good ... thoroughly competent people would be doing everything possible for his wife and children ... and so on. He, in his turn, started to re-state the situation as it appeared to him. Without the assistance of Brewer we might have been arguing the thing all afternoon.

'You heard what the Comp'ny Commander said!' Brewer suddenly fired. 'Salute! Right-turn! Quick march!'

That was that.

'It's a bit hard on these fellows,' I said when Taylor was out of earshot. 'Less than forty miles from their wives!'

Brewer performed the action I always thought of as 'sniffing at attention.' He said venomously, 'It's these perishin' women, if you ask me, sir. "Please come immediate!" What does she think he's joined—the League of 'Ealth an' Beauty?'

So I did not ask the Company Clerk to get me Taylor's home address till Brewer was out of the way.

I was summoned to London myself next morning: someone in Public Relations at the War Office seemed to think that a Company Commander would have time on his hands and wanted to fill it up for me. The interview was over before lunch, and I thought I might see for myself how Taylor's wife was getting on.

This, when the bus put me down at Lion Cross, did not appear so simple an undertaking. To the left of the main road an area of some ten acres looked rather like a West Indian township after the passage of a hurricane. Pitlock Street, the one I was searching for, was luckier than most

49

of its neighbours—it still existed; but all the houses on one side had been pushed over into the roadway. Here the authorities were certainly at work, police, rescue squads, ambulances. But it did not seem good sense to ask these tired and frantically labouring people if they could tell me the present whereabouts of Mrs Taylor of Number 23.

'The police station,' an old woman suggested. She was sitting on a pile of rubble, wearing a man's overcoat over a flannel nightgown and contentedly smoking a cigarette. 'They do say they've got all the names there, and where the people have been sent to. The station in Longmore Road, I mean.'

But as things turned out I did not have to go so far. Nearby, in Gaylor Street (I think it was), the rubble had been shovelled aside to make a passage just wide enough for vehicles to get through to the main road. Along this passage, as I reached it, came a small and very wobbly cart, so heaped with odds and ends that it looked like toppling over at every yard: there was an aged sofa, upside down, and several chairs; an ormolu clock, a bulging trunk, an array of kitchen tools and ornaments; in the midst of all this, a pair of toddlers sitting with their legs over the side and happily sharing a bag of sweets. In front (where the donkey should have been), a girl who might have been no more than seventeen was tugging manfully, with a third child of perhaps four years holding on to her skirt; while a pace ahead of her, in his undervest and battledress trousers, head down, shoulders thrusting against a length of chain between the shafts, was Taylor 08.

He caught sight of me before I could turn away; and for me it was a difficult moment. But not for him. With native wisdom, he evidently knew there were subjects which it is a waste of time to discuss. He faintly grinned.

'Had a bit o' luck, sir! Bloke I know over Turnham Green, I called to mind he had this barrer.' And then he laughed. 'Thought I'd take a loan on it—it's no use to Bert any more, he got himself blowed up. My nippers!' he added laconically, jerking his head. 'And this is Liz.'

I took the girl's place in the shafts—it seemed to be what manners demanded—while she continued to shove at the side. We went on, in that order, to the tram lines, and across by a route which Taylor knew to the Harrow Road.

'Yes, it was a lot o' luck, taking it all round, sir,' he said as we sweated through Willesden. ''Course, we lost a lot o' stuff—beautiful eidydown we lost, wedding present from Mum and Dad. But we got out quite a bit of it. Tidy job o' work, it was, haulin' it out from under all that muck.' (This I could see. His own and his wife's faces were mostly brick dust.) 'Nippers all right, too. Charlie, there, he thinks it's an extra bit o' holiday, don't you, Charlie!'

'But where are you making for?' I asked.

'Out Wembley. Got an ole auntie that way, she'll give Liz a doss, I reckon—a few days, anyway.'

'But you know,' I said, with belated severity, 'if you'd left the whole thing to the proper people they'd have moved your family to some really safe place in the country.'

Plainly he thought that foolish. He said, with an inflexion which made me think of J. D. Rockefeller, 'Yes—and what would've 'appened to all my property? Aw—they'll be right enough! Safe as 'ouses—Wembley.'

'And I think I ought to remind you,' I continued with some diffidence, 'that you're going to find yourself on a charge tomorrow. Absent without leave. That means loss of pay, and other things besides.'

He turned his head to give me a confidential glance. 'Them Jerries,' he said, summarising the situation as it seemed to affect us both. 'They're beginnin' to get on the awkward side of me!'

At dusk, after some six hours' hauling, we reached the aunt's road, and there I thought it well to leave them. To be honest, I don't think my legs or shoulders would have lasted another half-mile, that sweltering day.

'Very kind, I'm sure, Mister!' the girl said when I took my leave.

At which her husband reproved her: 'Oy, Liz, you say "sir" when it's an officer!' That much hold the Army had gained on Private Taylor.

He had the eldest child on his shoulders now; the other two were asleep, curled up amid the crockery. 'I'll get 'em fitted up,' he said largely, 'whether the ole girl like it or don't.' (He meant his aunt, I suppose.) 'Well, sir,' he added, with just a trace of shyness, 'I'll be seeing yer!' And I watched the mobile junk-shop creaking on, shakily but at a steady pace, till a bend in the road put it out of sight.

I asked Brewer next morning, 'Anyone for Company Office, Sergeant-Major?'

He replied, 'No charges this morning, sir.'

'Is Taylor 08 back?'

'Taylor 08, sir?'

'I had an idea he went absent yesterday.'

He seemed surprised.

'There's nothing from the Guard Room, sir. I'll ask the Platoon Sergeant—11 Platoon, that is. Dyson—find Sergeant Jacks an' bring him here. An' get a move on!'

Jacks came, and stood at attention.

'Taylor 08, was he on parade yesterday?' Brewer demanded fiercely.

There was just an instant's pause; and, glancing sideways, I saw a look pass between sergeant and sergeant-major! an Army look, delicately turned, packed tight with understanding. Then,

'On parade all day, sir!' Jacks said smartly.

Brewer, turning his stony face towards mine, showed

52

the expression of sterling honesty which is achieved only in a lifetime of artistic lying.

'Then that would be all right, sir?'

I said it would.

Later that day we were marching up a hill still steeper than the one near Marlow. I caught sight of a man who seemed to be half buried by his helmet; one whose tiny legs, matching their stride to that of the man in front, worked very lamely but with a slogging resolution. I came up beside him.

'How are the feet doing now?'

(This seemed as good as anything else to say. I had learnt that the discussion of some subjects is a waste of time.)

The grin which appeared was gone so quickly that I wondered afterwards if I had only imagined it.

'Feet, sir? Fine, sir! Nice walk in the country and the Army pays yer! Money for jam!' said Taylor 08.

R C Hutchinson

There's No Future In It

The nights he was not flying they would drive back late to the station, using her car. The flare-path would be laid; the lights on the hangars would shine like red stars in the winter darkness above the flat land. Sometimes the searchlights would be up, throwing a blue-white fire that fell widely like moonlight on the dark trees and hedges and on the winding road. They would sit in the car and, holding each other, talk for a long time. Frost on the very coldest nights would form like a silver collar on the glass of the windscreen and sometimes, on very still nights, he would wind down the window of the car and listen for a moment or two to the silence outside. She would lean her head on his shoulder and look upwards into the dark sky and then, listening too, hear the sound of the bombers coming home.

It did not seem to matter much that they were never likely to be married. He was rather small and compact, with fresh grey eyes that he sometimes did not seem able to focus correctly. He had 31 operational trips to his credit and all that seemed to matter was that he should continue coming back.

The morning afterwards, perhaps, he would ring the office. He would say simply, 'Hallo, dear, tonight.' She would try to remain calm, and later, perhaps, if operations were scrubbed, he would ring her again and she would find herself trembling as she put down the telephone, all her pretence of calmness gone.

She knew generally that he would be briefed in the early afternoon. He would take off about three o'clock or a little later and, according to the target, come back somewhere between eight and ten. It would often be too late to ring her after interrogation, but going to bed she would try to lie awake for the sound of the telephone. Sometimes she would fall asleep with the light still burning and would wake up in the small hours of the morning, bewildered and startled, not knowing where she was. Twice she fell half asleep and did not hear the telephone. Downstairs her father heard it, but after answering it, did not come to tell her who it was.

Her father was a rather big, grey-haired man with cheeks like loose pink rubber. He rolled his own cigarettes and it seemed to her that she never saw him without a newspaper. He rolled the cigarettes very badly—the tobacco fell wastefully on his clothes. The war had developed in him the latent qualities of the amateur strategist, and he always discussed the war while waving an untidy, wasteful cigarette. 'We ought to have cut the Tripoli road long ago. Long ago. You have only to look at the map. The same with the bombing of Berlin. What's gone wrong? Why aren't we over there more? Why aren't we over there night after night? Striking early and often is the decisive factor. You'd suppose it wouldn't escape our people.'

'Perhaps it's the weather,' she would say.

'Weather? There's another thing that beats me. Argue on simple lines, draw some absolutely logical conclusion which ought to be apparent to the merest child, and you always get the same answer. The weather! I don't doubt the weather is sometimes bad. But far from always, far from always. It's too often a convenient excuse—like the workman blaming his tools.'

'Nevertheless it nearly always is the weather.'

'Oh? Then what about last night? Clear moonlight like day. And was there a single operation? A couple of bombers over Brest.'

'You talk as if Brest were a seaside resort.'

'Look at the weather again to night. Magnificent. And in the morning what shall we hear? The same old story again, I suppose. A handful of bombers over Brest. Or nothing at all.'

'It's probably the most heavily defended place in Europe,' she said. 'It's just plain hell.'

'Kitty, Kitty,' her mother said. She looked up from her knitting, always khaki, and looked down again.

'Also I think you may find that tonight has been a big thing.'

'Oh! you know, do you?'

'No. Not exactly. I've an idea, that's all.'

'Ah! your pilot friend.'

She did not speak.

'You haven't brought him in lately.'

'No, dear,' her mother said.

'They spend most of their time out,' her father said. 'Somewhere.'

Her mother spoke without looking up from her knitting.

'Were you at the *Red Lion* last week?' her mother said. 'We heard you were there. Drinking with Air Force officers.'

'I was.'

'Is that the kind of place to be?' her father said.

'Drinking,' her mother said. 'It's not nice. Do you think so?'

'I want to be wherever he is.'

'Even there? Couldn't you give him up?' her mother said. 'He struck me as being older than he said. Do you know much about him? You are only twenty. It's all so terribly unsure. Perhaps he is married. Do you know?'

She did not answer.

'He looks older than twenty-four,' her mother said. 'Experienced. His eyes look old.'

She got up, calmly enraged, definite. 'He has done things that make him old,' she said, and went out of the room.

The following night they drove back late to the station. With the moon rising and the searchlights up, the road shone misty white between the dark hedges. The evening lay behind them, as always, simply secure; a few rounds of light ale at the *Red Lion*, the boys coming in group by group, the rounds growing, the crews mixing, sergeants with squadron leaders, gunners with navigators, warm broad Canadian voices mingled with English; and then the drive home, the blue lighting of the searchlights, and the moonlight throwing into relief the black winter trees, the hangars lit by red stars, the huge solitary dispersed aircraft in the fields; and lastly the silence after the car had stopped beyond the gate of the station.

'Was it a good trip, darling?'

He did not answer.

'Bad?'

'Pretty bad.'

'Did you have trouble?'

'The usual. Ten-tenths most of the way and then some hellish flak.'

She thought of her father. She saw him in an armchair, rolling the cigarettes, waving a newspaper. 'Always the weather!'

'I'm sorry I couldn't ring,' he said. 'It was late when we got in for interrogation. I didn't want to wake you.'

'I was awake,' she said.

They sat still, not speaking. She thought again of her father.

'Tell me about the trip.'

'Nothing to tell. Routine stuff.'

She did not like the sound of his voice, tired and guarded; the feeling that part of him was deliberately withheld.

'I can tell when you have trouble.'

'What trouble? No trouble at all.'

'Why have you got your hand in your pocket?' she said. 'You've had it there all the time.'

'All right,' he said.

He began suddenly to tell her something about the

57

trip. Though she had heard so much of it before, the awful significance of it was not lessened. He told her about the weather; ten-tenths, a bad storm soon after they turned for home, a spot of ice. 'They put up a hell's own flak at us. Just routine stuff, only a bloody sight worse. And they hit my hand. Took the skin off, that's all.' He kept it in his pocket.

She knew that he was not telling everything, that he never did, perhaps never would. Routine stuff, hellish flak, a spot of ice; the same words, the same repeated demand on courage, on fear if you like, the same holding back. She thought once more of her father: the world of the newspaper, the protest, the old indignations. To contrast it with the world of flak and ice, the long darkness of endurance, the spell of cold and strain 31 times repeated, was so difficult and angrily confusing that she said only, 'Does your hand hurt? Can I do anything for you?'

'Thanks, darling, I'm O.K.'

She remembered something.

'What time did interrogation finish? Why were you so late?'

'It wasn't so late. Not so very late.'

'If it wasn't so late why didn't you ring me?'

'I didn't want to wake you.'

'Tell me what happened,' she said.

He looked beyond the car window and said, 'We got a bit shot up. Just one of those things.'

'Bad?'

'Bad enough. A lump of flak blew a hole as big as a cartwheel in the starboard wing and the transmitter was u.s.* Shaky landing. But why pick on me? It happens every day.'

'Not to you.'

'It happens,' he said.

'You hate it, don't you?' she said.

* unserviceable

58

'Hate what?' he said.

'You hate going, don't you, time after time? The same place. The same job. The same everything. I know you hate it.'

'I hate it like hell,' he said. He looked beyond the car window again. The diffused lighting of the searchlights and the cloudy moon shone on the misted windscreen. The trees were black against it. 'But I hate what they're doing even more. That's what I really hate. What they do to me isn't half of what I mean doing to them. Not half. Not a quarter. Not a hundredth part. Is there anything wrong about hatred?'

She was thinking of her father, fussy with indignation, and she did not answer.

'It's good honest downright emotion, isn't it?' he said.

'Yes.'

'Sometimes I think we want more of it,' he said. 'God, sometimes I think we do.'

When at last she drove back from the station it was later than she thought. But at the house, to her surprise, her father and mother were still up. Her mother looked up from her knitting and her father looked at his watch.

'Either my watch is fast or it's ten past twelve.'

She did not speak.

'Even the *Red Lion* closes at ten.'

'It so happens I haven't been there.'

Her father coughed heavily. 'Does your pilot friend realise that we sit here, waiting?'

She did not answer.

'We have a right to be considered.'

She stood slowly taking off her gloves.

'You'll agree that he owes us something, won't you?'

She stood thinking of the long flight in the darkness, the hellish flak, the hole in the wing, the shell through the fuselage, the shaky landing; routine stuff; easy, nothing to tell, something done again and again. Her mind became unsteady with hatred. She looked at her

59

mother. The clean prejudiced hands were motionless on the knitting. Her father with the evening newspaper folded between his fingers stood with his back to the dying fire.

'Is he married?' her mother said.

'Does it matter?' she said.

Her father crackled the newspaper.

'My dear child, my dear child! Does it matter? I ask you. What about the future? Is there any future in that?'

'No,' she said; 'there's no future in it.'

She wanted to go on speaking, but her thoughts were disrupted and dispersed in the corners of her mind and she could not gather them together. She wanted to say why there was no future. She wanted to tell them about the flak, the darkness, and the bitter cold, about the way the tracer bullets came in at you so slowly that you could watch them until suddenly they hurled with red frenzy past your face, about the hatred and the monotony and the courage that was greater because it was rarefied by terror. She wanted to tell them that if there was any future it lay through this.

She went out of the room and went upstairs instead. She felt stifled by the warmth of the room downstairs and, not putting on the light, she opened the window and stood looking out. The air was bright with frost and the coldness struck with a momentary shock on her face and hands.

She stood there for a long time, looking out. The moon was going down beyond the houses. The searchlights were no longer up beyond the town. The sky was clear and calm and, as if there were no war and as it might be in the future, if there were a future, there was no sound of wings.

H E Bates

Silk for Lennie

MacKelland walked past the shop several times before he could muster courage enough to go in. His arms were laden with parcels for his folk in Scotland, neat packets of sugar, of butter, of cheese, of coffee and tea, and a pound of the best American tobacco for his father. He had put off another purchase to the last because, he told himself, it was the most important. This was true. But really he had put it off because he was young and shy, and the window of the stocking shop was full of other gauzy things that were charming enough but very alarming too.

At last, with a cautious glance in either direction, he dived inside. It was an early hour of the morning and there were only one or two women shoppers, for which he thanked his gods; but the place was well inhabited by wax figures in all stages of undress. Along the stocking counter stood at intervals a number of shapely but disembodied female legs displaying the things he sought.

A saleswoman approached. She was young and good-looking and poised, like most of the American girls he had seen, and she was smiling. She liked serving a man, unless he happened to be one of those sleek self-assured male creatures who bought gifts in lingerie shops with no more concern than a woman. This one was tall and very fair, with one of those clean skins that blush so easily. She had an amused notion that he was blushing all over and she liked him for it, and for his determined mouth and his embarrassed blue eyes.

'Something?' she said.

'Stockings,' blurted MacKelland, adding rather fiercely, 'for a lady.'

'Size? Colour?'

He put his parcels on the glass counter and rummaged in his pockets. He had got Lennie's size from her mother before leaving Glasgow, last voyage. He handed the saleswoman a slip of paper.

'It doesn't mention colour or weight,' she observed. And seeing his puzzled look, 'Perhaps I can help you. Tell me what she looks like. Is she old or young. Tall or short? And what's the colour of her eyes and hair?'

He drew in a full breath. It was easy to talk about Lennie.

'She's jimp—'

'Jimp?'

'Slim, you'd call it. She's twenty last birthday and comes up to about my shoulder. Her eyes are kind of brown, hazel's the word, and her hair's the colour of toffee only it's curly-like, but it has the same shine.'

'Um. What colours does she usually wear?'

He hesitated. 'Well, she's in the service, d'ye see, a corporal in the A.T.S.* That's khaki and they wear a dark sort of stocking, kind of thick. But this isn't for that. I mean, when my ship's in a home port Lennie—that's my girl's name—tries to get leave so we can spend a few days together at her mother's. She puts away her uniform then and wears things she had before the war. I don't know what colour they are. They look nice but when I'm with Lennie all I can see is her.' He added sheepishly, 'I suppose that sounds a bit daft.'

'I think it's beautiful,' said the young woman stoutly.

'So I want some silk stockings—not thick ones d'ye see? Because you can't get such things in Scotland now the war's on. And last leave I heard Lennie talking to her mother and saying something about stockings, about the A.T.S. ones, the way they made a girl feel, and how wonderful it'd be to have a pair of thin silk ones again, just the feeling of having them on.'

* Auxiliary Territorial Service

'And not the looks?'

MacKelland blushed gallantly. 'She has very nice legs.'

The young woman nodded as if this were the most sensible remark in the world.

'I think I can guess what she wants. How many pairs?'

'Could you spare six?'

He bolted out of the shop like a thief pursued. Congress Street was full of bustling people and he lost himself in the stream with a sigh of relief. If any chaps from the ship had seen him coming out of a place like that he could never live it down. A third mate was fair game. He walked through the snowy Portland streets to the docks with heavy arms and a light heart. The ship was taking grain, a good clean cargo and soon loaded. Tomorrow she would sail for Nova Scotia to join a convoy to Glasgow. Glasgow and Lennie!

The ship was as old as the hills. She had been dragged out of a Tyneside ship-knacker's yard when the war began and patched up to drag her weary hull about the seas again, like an old horse saved from the glue works by a sudden need for transport. McKelland had served his apprenticeship in a fast freight line and the old *Star of Maia* was rather a come-down, but he had just got his third mate's ticket and this was the first chance to use it. He looked upon her hogged grey hull with something like affection. For the past year she had carried him safely through all sorts of dangers when new ships were copping it right and left. And now she was taking him home to Lennie.

In the cabin he shared with Brundley, the second mate, he inspected the stockings with pride, keeping them in their transparent envelopes lest his hard hands start a thread in them. Flimsy things, marvellous things. He pictured Lennie's delight in them. With a queer hot beat in his throat he told himself that nothing was too good for her. And when he had his second mate's ticket and they could be married she should have everything she wanted, war or no war. So long as a ship floated and he in it, he would bring fine things home for Lennie.

He changed to his shabby sea uniform and went to cast a professional eye over the loading. The spouts from the elevator were still pouring grain like a yellow flood into the holds, but the shifting-boards would soon be out of sight and then the small space left under the hatches would be filled with bagged grain for a topping. She was pretty well down to her W.N.A.* mark and the steward and mess-boy were stowing the last stores. Topside, the wireless operators were tinkering with the lead-in insulator of their aerial wires. Aft, where the ship's gun pointed its lean finger over the stern, the naval gun crew were checking over the breech mechanism and the contents of the steel ammunition lockers. In the chartroom burly old Captain Llangollen was going over the ship's papers with the agent of the British Ministry of Shipping.

They sailed at sundown. The ship's destination was locked in the skipper's chest with his papers but everyone down to the messroom boy knew where they were going, and they knew what sort of gauntlet they would have to run. 'You have to go through hell to get to Heaven,' said the mate, a Glasgow man. The second mate had something else to say. Before turning in he tossed a coin and showed it to MacKelland with a grin. 'Heads! So it's pyjamas and comfort for Brundley. This night anyhow and maybe one night more.'

'You know the Old Man's orders about turning in,' MacKelland said soberly. 'Turn in all standing, that's the Word.'

'The Word's for boys and old men, chum.'

'I heard the agent tell the Old Man there'd been several ships bumped off in these waters in the past week.

* Winter North Atlantic

64

Now the Americans are in the war the subs are reaching out. The Old Man ...'

'The Old Woman! The old Welsh woman in the captain's clothes. Why, he's even got the de-Gaussing* gear switched on. I saw him on deck testing it the minute after we left the dock, squinting at his little pocket-compass, first to starboard, then to port, you know the way he does. Here! In sight of the American coast! D'you ever hear such bloody nonsense?'

Brundley was a tough bird of twenty-six with a hard blue jaw and a harder blue eye. He had been at Crete, and before that in the Limehouse docks during the big London blitz. Anything short of that was baby stuff.

Said he blithely, 'Look, Mac, we'll have to sleep in our clothes all the way from Halifax† to Glasgow, and that's long enough for Brundley. This side of Halifax Brundley's going to sleep like a blooming gentleman. In pyjamas.'

The *Star of Maia*'s weary old engines carried her on across the wide windy mouth of Fundy. When MacKelland came to turn in he did it war-fashion, according to the Word, fully clothed, blue kapok lifebelt under his head, boots and a flashlight within quick reach, cap and bridge coat on a handy peg.

The next day was bleak with an easterly wind and sea. From time to time snow squalls climbed blackly up the grey sky and killed all visibility with driving white stuff as hard as salt. Just before dusk they sighted the tip of Nova Scotia, a low point snow-covered and lit with the last yellow gleams of a February sunset. At eleven p.m. MacKelland was on the bridge, and Captain Llangollen with a pair of old-fashioned gold-rimmed glasses set far down his thick nose was poring over a mass of papers in the chartroom. The war seemed to have become a blitz of official documents. Captain Llangollen had dreams

* de-magnetising (as a protection against magnetic mines)
† a port in Nova Scotia

65

sometimes in which he saw himself drowning in a sea of papers. He called out through the door and MacKelland left his restless pacing of the dark bridge to enter the chartroom. The door-switch automatically plunged the room into darkness as soon as he opened it, and when he stepped inside and closed it the light came on blindingly. The Old Man blinked at him over the glasses.

Captain Llangollen looked tired. He looked an old man in truth. He had planned to retire in 1940 but the war had put all that aside. He and his wife came from the same village in Cardiganshire and they spoke Welsh in the home. His English had a strong accent. The cheeky messroom boy used to cock snooks at the Old Man's back when he was out of earshot and recite in a comic Welsh singsong, 'Do nott come down thatt ladder Missus Chones, for I haff taken itt a-way.' It was always good for a laugh. But they all liked the Old Man, and they knew the burden he carried.

'Eh,' he would sigh at the table, 'I am so glad I did most off my seafaring in times when a skipper's business wass to sail hiss ship. Nowadays *mawredd an'l** it iss a lawyer you haff gott to be.'

He said to MacKelland, 'You looked to the door switches today?'

'Ay, sir. They're all working properly, and we checked the porthole paint and all that. There's one thing, though, sir. The new galley stove. I noticed it tonight. There's a red glow when the draft-slots are open. And when we're changing watches and the men are going in and out with their cups of tea the galley door's open half the time. Of course I don't suppose that little glow could be seen very far.'

'Ah! But itt iss something, though, MacKelland, itt iss something. See the bosun in the morning and haff him make a canvas screen to hang inside the galley door. Be sure now! What iss the weather?'

*Welsh, meaning roughly 'good heavens'

66

'Very cold, sir. Not snowing any more but there's not much visibility, cloud over the stars.'

'Ah! Well, tomorrow we shall be in Halifax and I shall haff more paperss, more paperss. And you will see to that galley screen? Yess. That is all.'

MacKelland resumed his walking on the bridge, uphill and downhill with the ship's steady roll, passing and repassing the living statue of the seaman at the wheel. He paused frequently to stare into the night through the navigation slit in the armoured anti-aircraft screen. At regular intervals he cocked an eye at the glimmer-lit binnacle. It was cold on the bridge and he wore a lammy-coat* over his jacket, with the hood thrown back. The *Star of Maia* had been built for Mediterranean trade and in the frigid air of a still Canadian night her very bones seemed to crackle. A few minutes before midnight he paused again at the binnacle to check the course. Below he could hear the galley door opening and shutting as the next watch gathered for a mug-up before eight bells. Then it happened.

He could not remember the sound afterwards. He was conscious of a terrific shock that seemed to lift the ship bodily and heave it to port. He was flung off his feet in a headlong sprawling dive. He struggled to his knees. His head rang like a gong and his nose bled copiously. The helmsman was clinging to the wheel and saying something over and over, monotonously, in a voice as remote as the stars. Following the flash of explosives, vivid and terrible, which had lit the whole bridge for two seconds like a sheet of orange lightning, the darkness was something solid. MacKelland remained on his knees like a boxer hard hit and taking advantage of the count. The palms of his hands, flat on the deck, transmitted a tale of the ship's distress to his brain. The engines were dead. She had fallen off broadside to the swell and she rolled with a horrible lumpishness that became shorter and

*Sailor's thick, quilted coat

67

sicker at every swing. He could hear voices shouting somewhere, everywhere, and now he heard Captain Llangollen coming out of the chartroom and saw the bright cone of his flashlight.

'MacKelland!' said the Old Man.

'Ay, sir!' MacKelland pulled himself to his feet by the binnacle.

'Are you hurt?'

'All right, sir ... quite all right ... wind knocked out of me ... two torpedoes I think, sir ... struck almost together ... engine-room and somewhere about Number Two hatch ... rolling to port at the time ... must have blown the bottom out of her ...'

'Get to your boat then. Thiss iss no place—she's going fast. Go!'

As MacKelland fumbled for the flashlight in his lammy-coat pocket he heard the Old Man bellowing through the navigation slit, 'Abandon ship! All handss! Abandon ship! And God be with all!'

The lifeboats were on the bridge deck, two on the starboard side, two on the port. They were kept swung out on the davits, with their plugs in and gear lashed, ready for quick launching. MacKelland's was the after one on the starboard side. He flashed his torch towards the first, the captain's boat, and was startled to see nothing but the stem piece and a few shattered strakes dangling from one of the davits. It had hung right over the torpedo that hit the engine-room. His painful nose caught a whiff of burnt explosives. He ran towards his own boat and found half a dozen men pointing their torch beams over the side. The boat was intact but a flying chunk of metal had cut the launching tackle from the forward davit, and the boat hung up and down with its bow in the water, suspended by the after fall. There was a heavy swell and it thumped the dangling boat against the side unmercifully.

68

'Where are the others?' he demanded, flicking his torch over the men.

'Gone over to the port side,' one said. 'The mate's boat and the Second's are all right.'

'Get over there then, quickly. They'll find room for you.'

They vanished like wraiths around the corner of the wireless cabin. Sparks was in there, working furiously at the emergency apparatus in the dark.

With the disappearance of his boat's crew it occurred to the third mate that he had no more responsibility. Whatever he did now could affect nobody but himself, and the door to the officers' quarters, open and banging dismally, called to him like a voice. He dived inside and ran along the alley to the cabin he had shared with Brundley. It was a queer sight in the moving disk of his torch. Some freak of the explosions had pushed in the bulkhead to which the two berths were fastened. They were pinned to the deck. Yet on the remaining walls of the little coop their coats still hung, and the water carafe and glasses in the rack over the washbasin were in place and untouched. A moment's quick fumbling in a drawer and he turned to go. There was something queer about his feet. He turned the torch downward and noticed that he had lost his slippers in the sprawl on the bridge. He never wore boots on the bridge at night because they made such a racket when the Old Man was trying to catch a nap in the chartroom.

But now he noticed something else. He was standing in a little pool of blood, and the blood was not his own, it was coming in a thin warm trickle from under the collapsed bulkhead. He stooped and saw Brundley lying there with a long red gash in his scalp. Brundley apparently still sleeping—and in his pyjamas like a gentleman. Unconscious anyhow. And breathing. Mac-Kelland grasped the edge of the bulkhead and heaved. It moved, but not enough. He shouted for help. But that was hopeless. Everybody was busy getting the portside boats away and the ship was full of indescribable noises. One of these came from a cabin along the alleyway. MacKelland sprang into the passage and saw a flicker of light in the chief steward's room. He flashed his torch inside.

The steward was there, old Wortley, in shirt and trousers, with the braces dangling, his feet in a pair of carpet slippers, and with a blue life-jacket slung on wrong side foremost. In the light of the torch his thin hair stood up in a silver blur all round the bald top of his head. He had lost his glasses and he was trying to catch the black cat, Nig, which always slept in his berth.

'Come, Nig. Come, Niggie. Come on now!' coaxed the steward. He made enticing smacking sounds with his lips.

The cat's eyes glowed green from the berth. Its hair was on end. It looked black and enormous in the light of MacKelland's torch and the flaring match in the steward's hand. Wortley made a dive at the berth and the cat sprang, spitting, to the top of the wash-stand.

'Scared, 'e is,' observed Wortley over his shoulder. There was something odd in his voice. MacKelland turned his torch beam to the steward's face. Wortley blinked and put up a hand as if to brush the light away. MacKelland thought: *My God, he's mad.* He caught Wortley's shoulder.

'Come out of this, man! Come and help me ...'

'Without Nig?' Wortley said reproachfully. 'Not me! I ain't goin' without ol' Nig. Come Niggie now, ye bloody fool!'

MacKelland joined in the hunt, furiously, but it was Wortley who cornered the beast. The cat bit and scratched violently as he hugged it against his life-jacket.

'Now come on!' snapped MacKelland. As they ran along the passage there was a confused sound of voices from the port side, apparently from the boats. They were

70

yelling to Captain Llangollen on the bridge, 'Jump, sir, Jump!'

In the wrecked cabin the second mate had revived a little. They found him muttering something uncomplimentary about a woman at Barry Docks. They tugged at him but he was pinned fast. He swore at them thickly.

'Hold the light on him,' MacKelland said, passing the torch. He got down on his belly and crawled under the wreckage. Then, grunting, he braced himself upward with hands and knees, bearing the bulkhead with him. Something ragged-edged bit into his back cruelly and the sweat started all over him.

'Now?' he gasped.

'A bit more, sir,' Wortley said in an interested tone.

MacKelland shoved again. There was a rumbling below. The boilers? In a gust of despair he strained and felt the great weight moving with him. Wortley held the cat by the scruff of the neck and reached down with the other hand. Brundley's pyjama jacket tore and came away. The steward took another grip, this time under Brundley's naked shoulder, and with sudden strength dragged him out. MacKelland relaxed. The wreck of the bulkhead, which seemed to bear with it the whole hanging weight of the sinking ship, almost thrust him to the deck where Brundley had been. But not quite. He managed to squirm out, at the cost of his cap and a long tear in the back of his jacket. Between them, Wortley with a firm grasp on the cat, they got the mumbling second mate into the passage and out to the open deck. A sea leaped out of the darkness and burst over the rail. They went sprawling in a torrent of icy water, and MacKelland thought: *She's going. We're done for.* Then, miraculously, they were on their feet again, clawing at Brundley.

MacKelland shouted, 'We'll have to get him over to the port side where the boats are. Nothing here!' The ship was lurching downward, dying under their feet, and

71

the sounds of her last agony filled the night. The air forced out by the inrush of cold Atlantic was whistling and hooting through every crevice like a chorus of mad railway engines, and all over her things were slamming and uttering metallic shrieks. The seas one after another broke upon her upper works.

'Stick it, old girl,' muttered MacKelland. 'Give us another two minutes. Give us one!'

He heard Wortley's insane laugh. 'Look there!' the steward said. And there in the light of the torch, like a ghost, floating level with the rail and about one-third filled with water, was the third mate's boat. Some trick of the sea had kicked its bow upward and the thing had floated as the ship settled, still moored to the after davit by the slack ropes of the falls. They pitched Brundley in, and the cat after him, and MacKelland found the boat axe still in its beckets and hacked the falls away. The sea promptly carried the boat inboard, thumping her against the cabin bulkheads. The steward was fondling the cat. MacKelland yelled, 'Take an oar, man, and fend off, or we'll be sucked down with the ship!'

It was a terrible battle. The seas seemed to spring at them out of the night and the big boat was flung about like a chip. They persisted furiously. But it was the wind that saved them. It carried the boat along the side towards the bow. They drifted over the submerged forward well deck with a bump or two against the derrick posts in passing. They were clear, just to leeward, when they heard the boilers and the last bulkheads go. It was an anti-climax really after that frantic struggle. They could barely make out the upper works and the bridge against the faint haze over the stars, and the whole thing went down swiftly and vanished as an elevator disappears with its load beneath the floor of a department store. With something like a sob Mac-Kelland thought: *Good old Star, you went down like a lady at the end, no fuss, no kicking up the heels; and all that groaning and gasping at the last was just your way of saying, 'Good-bye, boys, I've got to go but I'll make it as easy for you as I can.'*

There was no sign of the other two boats. Probably the wind had carried them off to leeward. No use to hail. No good flashing a light, either. The U-boat was probably on the surface now, and watching somewhere off there in the dark. Wortley sat in the bow with his feet tucked up clear of the water sloshing about inside the boat, and with the cat held firmly in his arms.

'Good old Nig,' he kept saying. 'You're all right, Niggie boy, and so's old Wort, so long as 'e sticks to you, eh?'

MacKelland turned his attention to Brundley. The second mate was lying half drowned in the boat's bottom. He dragged the man into a sitting position with his back against a thwart. Then he rummaged for the bailer and flung out water until his arms ached. The boat drifted before the wind, rising and falling with the seas. It was not leaking badly, considering the pounding it had got, and as MacKelland persisted with his bailing the boat rode with some life.

Now in the sweep of that wind whistling along the sea's face in the dark it was cruel to be wet, as they all were, and fatal to be almost naked as Brundley was. The second mate was part conscious now, muttering, swinging his head to and fro, and shivering. MacKelland slipped off his lammy-coat and after a struggle managed to get Brundley into it, with Brundley chattering curses at him through the rattle of his teeth and demanding to be let alone. In the bow the steward hugged his cat for warmth.

'Ah, Niggie! Niggie!'

'Come and give me a hand to set the mast and sail,' snapped MacKelland. 'This wind's cold but it's fair for the Nova Scotia coast. And that's not far. We've a chance to make it afore we freeze to death.'

The sail was an old-fashioned dipping lug, easily managed, and when they got it set, the canvas filled with a brisk business-like flap in the dark. The boat began to move. There was no rudder and for lack of it MacKelland stood at the stern, steering with an oar. His feet were in the water that remained in the boat's bottom, but his feet did not feel so cold as the rest of him, exposed to that bitter wind.

'The land,' Wortley said. ''Ow far off would you say we are?'

'Fifteen or twenty miles. The Old Man was keeping in with the coast pretty well on account of the sub warnings.'

''Ow long will it take us to make it, d'you suppose?'

'Hard to say. Going with the wind and sea like this I'd say eight or ten hours.'

'We must be goin' faster'n that, Mac. Oh yes. A lot. Eh, Nig?'

'I don't think so. These lifeboats are heavy sailers at the best of times, and this one's partly waterlogged. I'd say we're making three knots at the best.'

'Ah well, we'll make it. Eh, Niggie—Niggie boy!'

MacKelland wondered how long a man could stay alive, wet and half clothed, in the cold of a Canadian winter night. The murky sky opened and shut from time to time and he got a glimpse of stars, but none that he could recognize. He continued to steer before the wind. As the hours went by he watched anxiously for light on the land, and there were moments when with a quick flutter of the heart he caught a glimmer on the crest of a sea far ahead; but always it turned out to be a star shining for the moment in a low gap in the ceiling, nothing more, and at each of these disappointments the cold seemed to penetrate a little more. He stooped to ply the bailer whenever he got a chance. The boat seemed to leak less as the night went on, and the slither of his steering-oar on the gunwale told him why. Ice was forming on the exposed upper strakes and sealing the opened seams. There were times when cold and weariness closed upon him and a monotonous voice that seemed to be a little way off in the darkness astern kept saying that it was hopeless, all of it, and that it would have been better to go down with the ship like Sparks and the Old Man and those shattered bodies in the engine-room and God knew how many of the others. But then he shook himself and braced his knees against the thwart and thought of Lennie.

At intervals he shook the second mate into movement, saying, 'Brundley! Can you hear me? Brundley! Say something!' After much shaking and shouting a mumble came from the depths of the lammy hood and he was satisfied. Once, returning to the oar, he felt the wind in another quarter and had a sudden choking fear. He checked it by a timely star-group, the first familiar thing in that strange night, and found that his fear was groundless, that the boat had merely fallen off while he was shaking Brundley, that the wind was still coming out of the east. He called out to Wortley, 'If the wind hauls, we're done.' The steward's voice came cackling out of the dark.

'Not with Nig we ain't. Never!'

The wind held and the night dragged out its last and longest hours. Daylight came, a thin grey stuff wandering up the overcast sky behind the boat, and after a time MacKelland made out ahead a long black shadow under the gloom that still hung in the west. He cried out to the others. The second mate muttered and stirred. The steward jumped up and held the cat above his head.

'See, Nig? There 'tis. There's the land. There's life for all of us. And all through you, my beauty! Old Wort knew, didn't 'e? Can't drown a cat, not a black 'un, till 'is lives run out, eh? And you've got seven left, Niggie, think o' that! One went in the *Carwood Castle*—blast them bloody 'Uns—and now there's one gone in the old

Maia—saved old Wort both times, didn't ye Nig? And seven left! Seven! Oh yes, there ain't a bloody submarine in 'Itler's navy that can drown old Wort so long 'e sticks to Niggie boy.'

'Shut up,' MacKelland said. 'Give the Second a hand; he's moving.'

The steward crept aft with the cat beneath his arm. He gave a hand to Brundley and the second mate came to his feet, swaying with the boat's heave and fall. 'God, I'm cold,' he muttered. 'Where are we?'

'There's the land ahead,' MacKelland said. 'Keep moving your arms and legs. Get your blood stirring. We'll have to scramble for it when the boat gets inshore. There'll be a surf with this wind.'

A black squall came up the sky behind them. Snow began to fly on the wind, a few white pellets that stung like birdshot and then a long thick gust that blotted out the land. Brundley and the steward huddled below the gunwale against the bite of it, with the cat between them. Grimly MacKelland stood at the oar, steering before the wind. The snow continued. There was nothing to be seen now but the foaming patch of sea in which the boat moved, and for lack of background, of anything to measure by, the lift and fall of each swell seemed tremendous and the boat itself seemed to be rushing on as if driven by silent and invisible engines towards destruction. The illusion was increased by the slant of the white stuff driving past, and the collective hiss of specks in millions striking on the skin of the sea all about him. Snow made a white crust on the sail and mast, on the inner strakes except where the water in the boat's bottom surged back and forth, on the thwarts, on the backs of the two men crouching under the gunwale, on his own breast and sleeves and trouser knees, all he could see of himself. He had a weird fancy that they were ghosts, all three of them, riding a ghost-ship in some cold hell.

At last the snowfall thinned and then stopped. The
76

patch of sea grew to an acre, to acres, and suddenly there was the land plain before them, the ominous white fling of surf where the long swells broke on the shore, a strip of snow-covered barren and then a dark mass of fir woods. There was no sign of habitation. Not even a break in the iron shore. There would be no chance to claw off, once the unwieldy boat got inshore. He wondered if he should try now to work along the coast for a better landing while he had a bit of offing. But his desperate inner mind said, *No. Get ashore.* That spell of snow was no mere squall. There's more behind. This easterly weather is working up a blizzard. Go in now, while you can see what you're doing, even if you have to swim for it at the end. Better that than be carried in willy-nilly further on, all blind in the snow.

He chose a spot where the lacy can-can of the surf did not fling itself with such abandon as elsewhere, and steered for that. When it entered the inshore surge the boat began to toss heavily. Their ears were filled with the crash of breaking seas.

'Strike the sail!' Wortley screamed. His old eyes bulged.

'And lose our steerage-way?' snapped MacKelland, busy with the oar.

He could see his chosen landing clearly now, a narrow finger of pebble beach, wet and steep, running up between two great boulders into the white of the land. The gap between the boulders was fairly wide but it was guarded by a ledge that appeared to be just awash, ten or a dozen fathoms out.

'Listen, Wort,' he shouted above the racket, 'the boat will strike that ledge you see whenever there's a back-wash. Probably swamp. Got to hang on, all of us. Next sea will lift her in to the beach. Then—can you hear me? —then we've got to grab the Second and get him up the shingle, clear of the sea. You understand? Never mind the cat. Nig can take care of himself.'

The shoreward rush of a big sea caught the boat and carried it on a curling white shoulder towards the gap. As it broke, the boat dropped and smote the ledge with great violence. It lifted and struck again farther in, and stove a hole in the port strakes towards the bow. The mast snapped, and Wortley clawed his way out from the sail. The boat filled. The men clung. The boat lifted, turned on its side in another cataract of white water, and spilled the men out. They grasped the gunwale. Above the boom and rattle of the surf they could hear the tough strakes smashing and felt themselves in the cold grasp of the sea. But still they clung. Then a wave exploded on the shore and threw them up the beach. The black cat sprang from Wortley's arms to safety in one long wild leap. The two men seized Brundley and staggered up the rattling wet shingle with the backwash sucking at their naked feet. Above tidemark they fell down together, gasping, in the snow. From the top of a boulder, strangely thin with its wet fur plastered to the skin, the black cat regarded them with great yellow eyes.

It was Wortley who recovered first. MacKelland heard him crying, 'Nig! Niggie! Where are you, my beauty? Don't 'ide, Nig. Don't 'ide from old Wort 'oo never done you any 'arm. Nig!' MacKelland got to his feet and looked about him. The cat was not to be seen.

'Help me get Brundley on his feet,' he said. 'We can't stay here.'

'Where are you going?' Wortley said plaintively.

'Up there in the woods. Some shelter there. Going to snow again soon. Come on.'

'Without my Nig?'

'To hell with Nig. Take Brundley's arm and come on.'

They moved off with the second mate between them. Brundley could not lift his head but he moved his legs like a drunken automaton. The head lolled to and fro with its red gash showing in the clotted scalp. The strip of barren between the shore and the woods was rugged

78

going. There was not much snow, but enough to hide the sharp edges of rocks amongst the low bushes, and the rocks and the harsh twigs cut the sodden white flesh of their naked feet. The first trees were poor stunted things, twisted by the sea winds. The trees became taller as they staggered on, and as they drew deeper into the woods they felt the wind no more. MacKelland was exhausted. Old Wortley was of little help in dragging the second mate along. They came to an opening amongst the trees and MacKelland halted.

'I'm afraid I've had it, Wort. Got to sit down. Rest a bit. Help me ease Brundley down. That tree-stump over there.'

They eased Brundley down on the stump, and the steward said, 'Don't sit down in the snow, Mister MacKelland. There's another stump over there. You go and brush the snow orf that 'un and sit there and get your breath, like. I'll 'old Mister Brundley 'ere.' Mac-Kelland swayed on his feet. The other stump invited him. It would be nice to lie down in the snow and rest his shoulders against it for a time. Get a bit of breath. Stop that pain in the lungs. Heart hammering. All that. Deserve a bit of a lie-down after all we've gone through. Why not?

'I think I'll lie down,' he said.

'I wouldn't if I was you,' old Wortley said. 'You'll never get up again, sir. Not in this world. Now you take these stumps, it's funny about these stumps. This 'un looks like it 'ad bin cut orf with a axe. But where's the tree? Where's the tree orf that 'un over there?'

Brundley lifted his head. 'Logs,' he said. 'Hauled 'em away. Any fool knows that.' It was so strange to hear him speak at all that they stared at the second mate incredulously. Brundley was shivering terribly and turning his head from side to side in the hood of the lammy-coat.

'There's no road,' MacKelland said.

'Horses,' Brundley said. 'Chains. Skid logs out to the

road. Worked in a lumber camp in Canada once. Jumped a ship, my first voyage. Seventeen. Know all about that.' His voice trailed off in a mumble.

MacKelland gazed about the clearing. 'These stumps aren't new. Last year, maybe. Where did they haul the log? Not up the slope, that's sure. Down that way somewhere. Looks like a bit of an opening through the trees. Come on let's get Brundley up and go that way.'

'Wot,' the steward said, 'and not a bit of arf-time?'

'Not till we drop,' MacKelland said. So they got Brundley up between them and staggered away down the slope, moving by instinct more than anything rational, choosing the easiest way amongst the boulders and the trees. At last they came to an old log-road running to right and left. They halted.

'Which way?' MacKelland said. 'We can't go on much longer.'

'Right,' Wortley said. And with one of his mad little cackles, 'You can't go wrong if you go right, can you?'

'Come on, then.' There was no sign of travel on the road. Bushes grew in it here and there. After a time they came around a bend and a gust of wind and snow blew in their faces. It's wrong, MacKelland thought. We're going back towards the sea. I won't say anything though. It's all hopeless. We've had it. Go on till we drop.

The road took them some distance back towards the sea and then turned to the left. MacKelland stopped.

'I've had it,' he said thickly. 'I'm going to drop, Wort.' A dark mist came and went before his eyes, a pattern of black specks shot with small red sparks.

'Wait a minute,' the steward said. 'Look there. Tracks.'

MacKelland could see nothing now. 'Man's?' he muttered without interest. Old Wort uttered a scream. 'Nao! Look! Look! It's a cat's. It's old Nig's. 'E knew! Trust old Niggie. 'E knew which way to go for grub and a nice warm bit o' fire. Come on, sir. It can't be far now, sir. Good old Nig!'

They stumbled on around the bend and came on a sudden hollow in the woods, cleared, with pole fences, and with a house, a small grey wooden house. There was a wisp of blue smoke from the chimney. They came down the slope shouting, dragging Brundley between them, Old Wort crying out that he could see a highway of some kind beyond the house, the marks of truck tyres in the snow—and Niggie, there was old Niggie right ahead. A man and a woman ran out of the house and came towards them.

There was warmth, delicious and stupefying, close against his skin and all about him, and a great pain in his hands and feet. His feet seemed to be on fire. He opened his inflamed eyes and saw a man in shirt-sleeves doing something at the foot of the bed. He tried to lift himself on his elbows and could not.

'Hello,' the man said, 'that's a pretty pair of feet you've got.'

'Doctor?'

'That's right. I came out as soon as they got word to Liverpool.'

'Liverpool?'

'Not the one you're thinking about. This one's in Nova Scotia. We'll shift you in there tomorrow.'

'My feet. My hands.'

The doctor saw the fear and the begging in MacKelland's eyes.

'They're bad, but I think they'll come around with proper treatment. You've got a bad case of what we call 'immersion foot'—we've had a lot of torpedoed crews this winter—and frostbite on top of that, and in your hands. I don't know how or where you travelled after you got ashore but your feet look as if they'd tramped all over a dump of old razor blades. What happened?'

'Never mind that. The others—'

'As well as you could expect. That fellow with the cut

81

head's got a bad case of shock as well as exposure and frostbite but I think he'll pull round in time. As for the old chap, he's as mad as a hatter but the most cheerful lunatic I ever saw. Keeps nursing and talking to a big black cat. Says it saved your lives.'

'That's right,' MacKelland said.

'Ah, but the other chap in his conscious moments keeps insisting it was you. Says when the ship was going down you deliberately went inside to get him out, and that balmy steward too. Says you got 'em both into a boat, and that you—you alone—brought the boat to shore. Calls you a bloody hero and says there wasn't another man in the ship who would or could have done it.'

'No,' the third mate said. 'He's quite wrong. What I went back for was something else.' He paused, and his blue eyes opened very wide. 'Doctor!'

'Yes?'

'My jacket—I see it hanging there on the wall. In the right-hand pocket. There should be a package. Will you see if it's all right?'

The doctor went to the jacket and fumbled in the pockets.

'Here it is—in the left-hand one, not the right. Paper's wet and torn but there seems to be an inside wrapper. Cellophane. And—hello! Stockings! Six pairs of silk stockings!'

'For Lennie—for my girl,' MacKelland said, staring at the ceiling. There was a silence. The doctor regarded him curiously.

'So you see,' the third mate said, 'I'm not a hero after all.'

The doctor turned the cellophane packets in his hands. 'Because you went back for these? I see. If you'd been thinking simply of yourself, and the sea, and the cold, you might have gone back for your boots, or a couple of sweaters, or blankets, or anything but silk stockings. But you thought of nothing but these things for what's-her-name. And while you were getting them you happened to find the steward and the other chap, not to mention the cat. So you're not a hero. Of course you're not. You're a damned fool.'

The doctor paused and regarded the twisted smile on MacKelland's face, on the cracked and brown-scabbed lips, and the bloodshot blue eyes that stared at the ceiling and saw nothing but a girl in Glasgow.

'But you're the kind of fool that makes this world go round.'

The third mate shook his head a little and closed his eyes. This doctor with the Canadian accent that sounded a little Scotch seemed a decent chap, and no doubt he was very wise in his profession. But he was the fool himself. He didn't know that it was the Lennies who made the world go round.

Thomas H Raddall

The Enthusiastic Prisoner

Henry Holden decided to get an Italian prisoner-of-war after he had seen several at work on Esmond's farm. Esmond was building a shed, and it was beautiful to see how they rushed to carry anything he picked up, and how they seemed to take it for granted that they were there to do all the heavy work while the boss gave the orders.

When the captain in charge of the P.O.W.C.C.* had a preliminary look over Henry's place he tactlessly asked him if he were an invalid; he saw so few signs of work being done and so many of neglect. He wasn't at all keen on letting Henry have a P.O.W.; he didn't think he was the type to handle them successfully, but on the other hand, he was eager to get his 'hundred'.

When the P.O.W. arrived Henry was decidedly disappointed with him at first sight.

He did not look obliging and polite; he didn't even look like an Italian. He had a tremendous amount of fuzzy brown hair, his eyebrows were so large and dense they nearly surrounded his eyes and thick hair grew all round his neck and jutted out of his ears. His small bright eyes glinted sharply from among all the hair, not at all like the large, soft and servile eyes of the Italians at Esmond's.

In fact, he reminded Henry of a big brown bear, with his air of having great physical strength and tremendous determination. When the military truck drove away Henry had an uncomfortable feeling of having let himself in for something.

He directed Pietro to his room and, while he was

*Prisoner-of-war control centre

settling in, tried hurriedly to work out a plan of what to do with him. There was, of course, plenty of work to be done, but it wasn't easy to start a man who didn't understand English, or know Australian farms. In a few minutes Pietro appeared.

'Worrk,' he said briefly and determinedly.

Henry abandoned his half-formed plan to let Pietro have the first half-day off. He thought of a number of jobs, only to realize that he didn't have the necessary materials. In desperation he decided to repair a fence. He pointed to the fence and to some tools and tried to explain to Pietro.

'Unnerstan', *reparare*,' said Pietro.

He picked up a shovel and pick, and starting hunting for a '*leva*'. Henry soon realized that he meant a crowbar, but he couldn't remember where his was. Pietro looked at him in astonished reproval. When they started off Pietro carrying all the heavy tools while Henry carried the wire-strainer, Henry felt better, though he was sure Esmond's men would have offered to carry the wire-strainer, too.

They did little good with the fence, though Pietro was obviously eager to work. It really needed a lot of new posts and wires and Henry had neither. They tightened what wires were there and braced and stayed some of the key posts in a makeshift manner. Pietro liked the wire-strainer. Apparently he had never seen one before, and was greatly intrigued with the way it worked.

'Very ni', very ni',' he said.

But when they were going home for dinner he glanced disapprovingly at the propped-up posts. 'No good, no good.'

After dinner, Henry usually had a nap that lasted well into the afternoon if the day happened to be warm, but Pietro apparently didn't know about dinner hours. He waited outside the door for a while then knocked and said, quite politely but very firmly, 'Worrk.'

Henry went out, and remembered the woodheap. It cheered him immensely. He had recently brought in a load and it would take Pietro several days to chop it up. It would be a great standby. Pietro could work there all the afternoon.

He lay down while Pietro chopped with great vigour, but he could not sleep or even relax properly because of his problem. His wife and family, too, kept asking him questions; they were rather awed by Pietro.

He heard the rumble of the wheelbarrow on the veranda several times and sounds of cut wood being tipped out. Then Pietro knocked on the door. He pointed to the great pile of wood and said, '*Sufficiente.*'

'No, not sufficient,' said Henry. 'Chop more.'

Pietro looked at him with a blank expression.

'No unnerstan',' he said, and before Henry could work out another way of expressing himself, he inquired, '*Sufficiente* one day? Two day? T'ree day?'

'T'ree day,' Henry admitted reluctantly.

Pietro smiled broadly and looked surprisingly pleasant as he did so. 'Plenty sufficient,' he said, closing the argument.

Henry went and got his hat. He could hear the wind banging a loose sheet of iron on the roof of the machinery shed. They would begin by nailing it down. But when they climbed the roof Pietro discovered that half the sheets were loose. Henry gave him the nails and directed him to nail down the flapping sheet. But Pietro was hunting round for causes. He discovered that the rafters were rotting and demonstrated it by giving one a hard hit with the hammer. It split from end to end and a couple of sheets immediately blew off the roof.

They spent the afternoon cutting trees in the scrub and trimming them for rafters, though nothing had been farther from Henry's intention and inclination. He cut down a few little trees while Pietro cut a lot of big ones. Pietro always took the heavier end when they loaded the rails, but even so Henry became exhausted. Round about four o'clock he decided to go home.

'Sufficient,' he said.

Pietro consulted a diagram he had made.

'No sufficient,' he said. '*Ancora* four.'

They went on working.

At tea that night Pietro met all the family. There were a flapper daughter, three younger boys, and a baby. He was particularly interested in the baby.

He made some queer foreign noises at it, and to everyone's surprise it showed unmistakable signs of affection for him. He asked Mrs Holden if it were breast-fed, and when she told him, in some confusion, that it was not, he wanted to know why. Then he gave her detailed and intimate directions, mainly by signs, about how to ensure an abundant flow for the next baby. The flapper daughter half smothered a lot of embarrassed giggles, and the boys nearly 'busted' trying not to laugh. Henry felt that he should reprimand Pietro for his indelicacy, but didn't know how he could make him understand.

The next day Henry felt stiff and sore. He decided to relax, but Pietro kept calling him onto the roof, sometimes for advice, but mostly to help him in fitting rafters which were too big to be '*possibile solo*'.

They finished re-roofing the shed by the week-end. Pietro wanted to know if they would cut some fenceposts next week to repair the fences. Henry thought of how he would suffer if he had to work on the other end of a cross-cut saw with a tireless bear like Pietro. 'No,' he said, 'some other work.'

But he didn't like the way Pietro looked at him, so he decided to hide the cross-cut saw.

On Sunday Esmond's Italians came to visit Pietro, and told him all about what was going on at their place. On Monday morning Pietro wanted to know why Henry was not preparing his soil for his crops like Mr Esmond. Henry looked a bit guilty, then tried to explain that he used different methods from Esmond. Pietro was not satisfied.

'Mr Esmond good *resultati?* No good *resultati?*'

Henry had to admit that Esmond's results were good. He also had to confess that his results were often bad.

'*Provare* similar Mr Esmond,' Pietro suggested enthusiastically. '*Possibile* very good oat, very good weet.'

'Tractor broken,' said Henry. He was always overwhelmed by a feeling of hopeless apathy in the autumn and he couldn't face the strain of all the preparations necessary for his worn-out plant.

'Me look?' asked Pietro, and was off before Henry could say anything.

Pietro had a thorough look over the tractor and scarifier. He made a list of all the new parts needed, which he laboriously translated into English with the help of his little dictionary. He explained that he was not a mechanic, but he had had a lot of experience with military vehicles.

He suggested that Henry go to town and buy the necessary parts, and Henry went, glad to escape from the responsibility of Pietro for an afternoon. While Henry was away Pietro 'polished' the toolshed and the farmyard.

When Henry came home, rather late in the evening and somewhat the worse for wine, he thought he had come to the wrong farm until Pietro emerged and carried his parcels for him. He was in an exalted mood and gave Pietro an orange for his services. But Pietro spoiled the effect by telling him several things he had forgotten to bring.

At the table that night Pietro objected to Mrs Holden giving the baby honey to stop it crying.

'No good 'oni, no good,' he said.

She continued to exercise the lawful rights of a mother. Suddenly the baby vomited. Pietro made an angry noise, jumped up, and put the honey-pot away in the cupboard.

'No good, no good,' he said so emphatically that she was startled and impressed.

Henry found that he couldn't tell Pietro much about overhauling farm machines. He stood by to explain where tools, parts, and materials were kept, but frequently found it easier to fetch them than to explain; sometimes when Pietro was held up he became so impatient that Henry found himself running just like one of Esmond's Italians, until he remembered his dignity as a *padrone*.

They had an auspicious rain when everything was ready, and Henry's land was never worked into better condition.

The tractor ran very well. Pietro assumed a jealous control of it, and appeared to be perfectly happy on it no matter how long he worked. The arrangement suited Henry excellently.

He felt free for the first time since his prisoner arrived. He had plenty of time to turn over all the vague plans forming in his head.

When Pietro finished working the land he suggested again that they cut some fence-posts. But Henry was ready with his own plan. Pietro was to paint the house. Pietro agreed heartily; the house certainly needed painting. They went to have a good look at it. Not only had the paint peeled off, but much of the plaster was cracked and loose.

'No good paint,' said Pietro. '*Prima* plaster.'

The thought of all the work and expense involved in plastering horrified Henry.

He said, authoritatively, 'Paint sufficient', and took a trowel and demonstrated how the rough plaster could be smoothed off.

He handed the trowel to Pietro, who made what appeared to be a similar movement. But the result was vastly different, at least a wheelbarrow-load of plaster fell off the wall.

'Plenty similar,' Pietro said, and knocked off another square yard. Henry gave in.

Henry was kept very busy mixing and carrying plaster to Pietro. It had to be mixed in small lots and applied immediately, Pietro said, otherwise it would fall off just like the previous plaster.

When the job was finished Henry brought out the paint. Pietro was very interested in the '*colore*'. When he discovered that it was to be a drab, uniform stone-colour all his eagerness vanished.

'No good, no good,' he said. 'Similar mud.'

He wouldn't take the brush when Henry offered it to him.

'Brush no good,' he said. '*Troppo* old.'

Henry tried the brush and had to admit it was worn out. He decided to go to town and buy a new one. Pietro wanted to go, too, to have his hair cut. Henry left him at the Control Centre and went to do his shopping.

When he walked into the general store where he did most of his business he had an uneasy feeling that he was being followed. He turned and saw Pietro carrying the two big cans of stone-coloured paint. He had that brown-bear look about him which Henry hadn't liked the first time he saw him.

The manager of the hardware store came up to them. He saw by the expression in Henry's eye that he wasn't sure of himself, so he turned to Pietro, who appeared to know exactly what he wanted. Pietro held up the tins.

'*Colore* no good,' he said.

The manager remembered having advised Henry against a uniform drab colour, and immediately set out to help Pietro. He quite ignored Henry's somewhat indistinct, 'No, it's all right. I'll keep it.'

He showed Pietro a colour-card, from which he selected a very light cream, bright blue, and a black.

'One big creama, one little blue, one little little *nero*,' he said.

90

The manager was, as he would have said, intrigued. He tried to discover what design Pietro had in mind, and Pietro demonstrated as best he could, attracting a lot of attention from other shoppers, who began to gather round.

Henry became most uncomfortable. 'I won't have it at any price,' he protested. 'Everyone who goes past will die laughing.'

'Ah, garn!' said a big voice from the back. 'Let him have a go. It couldn't look any worse than it's looked for the last twenty years.'

Then a couple of ladies joined in.

'How interesting!' said one. 'The Italians are so artistic, aren't they?'

The other one said, 'I remember seeing the adorable Italian cottages painted just like that. You must let us come and see it, Mr Holden.' She happened to be the wife of Henry's long-suffering mortgagee, and her word carried some weight with him. Quite a number of others voiced favourable opinions before Henry and Pietro carried out the cream, blue and black paint.

Pietro took endless pains over the painting, and all the time he was at it Henry felt resentful, despite the fact that many people came and admired it. He comforted himself by compiling a long list of heavy jobs Pietro would have to do when he was finished. He had the interpreter prepare a translation and when at length the house was finished he gave Pietro a week's programme, consisting mainly of firewood-carting and post-hole digging.

But that day it rained, a splendid soaking rain, and during the night it cleared.

Henry was awakened early in the morning by the roar of the tractor starting. He was puzzled and rather annoyed; Pietro was up to something. Then he realized that Pietro had made the all-important decision of the year, to start sowing the wheat.

Henry thought, with some indignation, of the programme he had given Pietro, but he also realized that it was much more important to have the wheat sown while the soil was moist. He lay thinking for a long time of ways in which he could reassert himself, and all the time he heard the noises of Pietro's preparations. He stayed there because he always hated the worry of working out the proportions of wheat and fertilizer and adjusting the machines accordingly, and all the other important details necessary for a successful sowing season.

When at last he went out Pietro hurried up to him, his face aglow with enthusiasm.

'Oh, rain very nice!' he said. '*Possibile* very good weet this year, similar Mr Esmond.'

He pointed to the tractor hitched to the sowing combine and the farm cart loaded with supplies of seed, fertilizer, and tractor fuel.

'After brekfus I take tractor and weet machine. You bring *carro*. *Allora* we commence before Giuseppe and Leonardo on farm Mr Esmond.'

'Yes, Pietro,' said Henry.

E O Schlunke

Benny, the War in Europe, and Myerson's Daughter Bella

When Benny was sent overseas in the autumn of 1941 his father, Mr Garber, thought that if he had to give up one son to the army, it might as well be Benny who was a quiet boy, and who wouldn't push where he shouldn't; and Mrs Garber thought: 'My Benny, he'll take care, he'll watch out'; and Benny's brother Abe thought 'when he comes back, I'll have a garage of my own, you bet, and I'll be able to give him a job.' Benny wrote every week, and every week the Garbers sent him parcels full of good things that a Jewish boy should always have, like salami and pickled herring and *shtrudel*. The food parcels were always the same, and the letters—coming from Camp Borden and Aldershot and Normandy and Holland—were always the same too. They began—'I hope you are all well and good'—and ended—'don't worry, all the best to everybody, thank you for the parcel.'

When Benny came home from the war in Europe, the Garbers didn't make much of a fuss. They met him at the station, of course, and they had a small dinner for him.

Abe was thrilled to see Benny again. 'Atta boy,' was what he kept saying all evening, 'Atta boy, Benny.'

'You shouldn't go back to the factory,' Mr Garber said. 'You don't need the old job. You can be a help to your brother Abe in his garage.'

'Yes,' Benny said.

'Let him be, let him rest,' Mrs Garber said. 'What'll happen if he doesn't work for two weeks?'

'Hey, when Artie Segal came back,' Abe said, 'he

93

said that in Italy there was nothing that a guy couldn't get for a couple of Sweet Caps.* Was he shooting me the bull, or what?'

Benny had been discharged and sent home, not because the war was over, but because of the shrapnel in his leg, but he didn't limp too badly and he didn't talk about his wound or the war, so at first nobody noticed that he had changed. Nobody, that is, except Myerson's daughter Bella.

Myerson was the proprietor of Pop's Cigar & Soda, on Laurier Street, and any day of the week, you could find him there seated on a worn, peeling kitchen chair playing poker with the men of the neighbourhood. He had a glass-eye and when a player hesitated on a bet, he would take it out and polish it, a gesture that never failed to intimidate. His daughter, Bella, worked behind the counter. She had a club foot and mousy hair and some more hair on her face, and although she was only twenty-six, it was generally supposed that she would end up an old maid. Anyway she was the one—the first one—who noticed that the war in Europe had changed Benny. And, as a matter of fact, the very first time he came into the store after his homecoming she said to him: 'What's wrong, Benny? Are you afraid?'

'I'm all right,' he said.

Benny was a quiet boy. He was short and skinny with a long narrow face, a pulpy mouth that was somewhat crooked, and soft black eyes. He had big, conspicuous hands, which he preferred to keep out of sight in his pockets. In fact, he seemed to want to keep out of sight altogether and whenever possible, he stood behind a chair or in a dim light so that people wouldn't notice him—and, noticing him, chase him away. When he had failed the ninth grade† at Baron Byng High School, his class-master, a Mr Perkins, had sent him home with

* a type of cigarette sold in North America
† a class for fourteen-year-olds

94

a note saying: 'Benjamin is not a student, but he has all the makings of a good citizen. He is honest and attentive in class and a hard worker. I recommend that he learn a trade.'

And when Mr Garber had read what his son's teacher had written, he had shaken his head and crumpled up the bit of paper and said—'A trade?'—he had looked at his boy and shaken his head and said—'A trade?'

Mrs Garber had said stoutly, 'Haven't you got a trade?'

'Shapiro's boy will be a doctor,' Mr Garber had said.

'Shapiro's boy,' Mrs Garber had said.

And afterwards, Benny had retrieved the note and smoothed out the creases and put it in his pocket, where it had remained. For Benny was sure that one day a policeman, or perhaps even a Mountie, would try to arrest him, and then the paper that Mr Perkins had written so long ago might prove helpful.

Benny figured that he had been lucky, truly lucky, to get away with living for so long. Oh, he had his dreams. He would have liked to have been an aeroplane pilot, or still better, to have been born rich or intelligent. Those kind of people, he had heard, slept in mornings until as late as nine o'clock. But he had been born stupid, people could tell that, just looking at him, and one day they would come to take him away. They would, sure as hell they would.

The day after his return to Montreal, Benny showed up at Abe's garage having decided that he didn't want two weeks off. That pleased Abe a lot. 'I can see that you've matured since you've been away,' Abe said. 'That's good. That counts for you in this world.'

Abe worked very hard, he worked night and day, and he believed that having Benny with him would give his business an added kick. 'That's my kid brother Benny,' Abe used to tell the cabbies. 'Four years in the infantry, two of them up front. A tough hombre, let me tell you.'

For the first few weeks Abe was very pleased with Benny. 'He's slow,' he thought, 'no genius of a mechanic, but the customers like him and he'll learn.' Then Abe began to notice things. When business was slow, Benny— instead of taking advantage of the lull to clean up the shop—used to sit shivering in a dim corner, with his hands folded tight on his lap. The first time Abe noticed his brother behaving like that, he said: 'What's wrong? You got a chill?'

'No. I'm all right.'

'You want to go home, or something?'

'No.'

Then, when Abe began to notice him sitting like that more and more, he pretended not to see. 'He needs time,' he thought. But whenever it rained, and it rained often that spring, Benny was not to be found around the garage, and that put Abe in a bad temper. Until one day during a thunder shower, Abe tried the toilet door and found that it was locked. 'Benny,' he yelled, 'come on out, I know you're in there.'

Benny didn't answer, so Abe got the key. He found Benny huddled up in a corner with his head buried in his knees, trembling, with sweat running down his face in spite of the cold.

'It's raining,' Benny said.

'Benny, get up. What's wrong?'

'Go away,' Benny said. 'It's raining.'

'I'll get a doctor, Benny. I'll . . . .'

'Don't—you mustn't. Go away. Please, Abe.'

'But Benny . . . .'

A terrible chill must have overcome Benny just then for he began to shake violently, just as if an inner whip had been cracked. Then, after it had passed, he looked up at Abe dumbly, his mouth hanging open. 'It's raining,' he said.

96

His discovery that afternoon gave Abe a good scare, and the next morning he went to see his father. 'It was awful spooky, Paw,' Abe said. 'I don't know what to do with him.'

'The war left him with a bad taste,' Mrs Garber said. 'It made him something bad.'

'Other boys went to the war,' Abe said.

'Shapiro's boy,' Mr Garber said, 'was an officer.'

'Shapiro's boy,' Mrs Garber said. 'You give him a vacation, Abe. You insist. He's a good boy. From the best. He'll be all right.'

Benny did not know what to do with his vacation, so he tried sleeping in late like the rich and the intelligent, but in the late morning hours he dreamed bad dreams and that made him very frightened so he gave up that kind of thing. He did not dare go walking because he was sure that people could tell, just looking at him, that he was not working, and he did not want others to think that he was a bum. So he began to do odd jobs for people in the neighbourhood. He repaired bicycles and toasters and lamps. But he did not take any money for his work and that made people a little afraid. 'Isn't our money good enough for him? All right, he was wounded, so maybe *I* was the one who shot him?'

Benny began to hang around Pop's Cigar & Soda.

'I don't like it, Bella,' Mr Myerson said, admiring the polish of his glass eye against the light. 'I need him here like I need a cancer.'

'Something's wrong with him psychologically,' one of the card players said.

But obviously Bella liked having Benny around, and after a while Mr Myerson stopped complaining. 'Maybe the boy is serious,' he thought, 'and what with her club-foot and all that stuff on her face, I can't start picking and choosing. Beside, it's not as if he was a crook!'

Bella and Benny did not talk much when they were together, afraid, perhaps, that whatever it was that was

97

'starting' up between them, was rich in delicacy, and would be soiled by ordinary words. She used to knit, he used to smoke. He would watch silently as she limped about the store, silently, with longing and burning hope and consternation. The letter from Mr Perkins was in his pocket. He wanted to tell her about the war —about things.

'I was walking with the sergeant. He reached into his pocket to show me a letter from his wife when . . . .'

There he would stop. A twitching would start around his eyes and he would swallow hard and stop.

Bella would look up from her knitting, waiting for him the way a mother waits for a child to be reasonable, knowing that it is only a question of time. But Benny would begin to shiver, and, looking down at the floor, grip his hands together until the knuckles went white. Around five in the afternoon he would get up and leave without saying a word. Bella would give him a stack of magazines to take home and at night he would read them all from cover to cover and the next morning he would bring them back as clean as new. Then he would sit with her in the store again, looking down at the floor or at his hands, as though he were in great pain. Time passed, and one day instead of going home around five in the afternoon he went upstairs with her. Mr Myerson, who was watching, smiled happily. He turned to Mr Shub and said: 'If I had a boy of my own, I couldn't wish for a better one than Benny.'

'Look who's counting his chickens already,' Mr Shub said.

Benny's vacation continued for several weeks and every morning he sat down in the store and stared at his hands, as if he expected them to have changed overnight, and every evening he went upstairs with Bella pretending not to have heard the remarks, the good-natured observations that had been made by the card-players as they passed.

98

Until, one afternoon she said to him: 'I'm going to have a baby.'

'All right,' Benny said.

'Aren't you even going to say luck or something?'

Benny got up and bit his lower lip and gripped his hands together hard. 'If you only knew what I have seen,' he said.

They had a very simple wedding without speeches in a small synagogue and after the ceremony was over Abe slapped his younger brother's back and said: 'Atta boy, Benny. Atta boy.'

'Can I come back to work?'

'Sure, of course you can. You're the old Benny again,' Abe said. 'I can see that.'

And when Mr Garber got home, without much more to expect but getting older, and more tired earlier in the day, he turned to his wife and said: 'Shapiro's boy married into the Segals.'

'Shapiro's boy,' Mrs Garber said.

Benny went back to the garage but this time he settled down to work hard and that pleased Abe a good deal. 'That's my kid brother, Benny,' Abe used to tell the cabbies, 'married six weeks and he's already got one in the oven. A quick worker, I'll tell you.'

Benny settled down to work hard and when the baby was born he even laughed a little and began to save money and plan things, but every now and then, usually when there was a slack period at the garage, Benny would shut up tight and sit in a chair in a dark corner and stare at his hands. Bella was good with him. She never raised her voice to say an ugly thing, and when he woke up screaming from a dream about the war in Europe she would stroke his neck and say tender things. He, on the other hand, began to speak to her confidentially.

'Bella?'

'Yes.'

'I killed a man.'

'What? You what? When did you . . . .'

'In the war.'

'Oh in the war. For a moment I—a German you mean . . . .'

'Yes, a German.'

'If you ask me it's too bad you didn't kill a dozen. Those Germans I . . . .'

'I killed him with my hands.'

'Go to sleep.'

'Bella?'

'Yes.'

'Are you ashamed that I . . . .'

'Go to sleep.'

'I saw babies killed,' he said. 'What if . . . .'

'There won't be another war. Don't worry about our baby.'

'But . . . .'

'Sleep. Go to sleep.'

The baby grew into a fine, husky boy, and whenever there was a parade Benny used to hoist him on his shoulders so that he could see better. He was amazed, truly amazed, that he could have had such a beautiful child. He hardly had nightmares at all any more and he became talkative and somewhat shrewd. One night he came home and said: 'Abe is going to open a branch on Mount Royal Street. I'm going to manage it. I'm going to be a partner in it.'

So Benny finally threw away the paper that Mr Perkins had written for him so long ago. They bought a car and planned, the following year, to have enough money saved so that Bella could go to a clinic in the United States to have an operation on her club foot. 'I can assure you that I'm not going to spend such a fortune to make myself beautiful,' Bella said, 'and plainly speaking I'm not doing it for you. But I don't want that when the boy is old enough to go to school that he should be teased because his mother is a cripple.'

Then, a month before Bella was to go to the clinic, they went to see their first cinemascope film. Now, previous to that evening, Bella had made a point never to take Benny along to see a war film, no matter who was playing in it. So as soon as the newsreel came on—it was that special one about the hydrogen bomb tests— she knew that she had made a mistake in bringing Benny with her, cinemascope or no cinemascope. She turned to him quickly. 'Don't look,' she said.

But Benny was enthralled. He watched the explosion, and he watched as the newsreel showed by means of diagrams what a hydrogen bomb could do to a city the size of New York—never mind Montreal.

Then he got up and left.

When Bella got home that night she found Benny huddled up in a dark corner with his head buried in his knees, trembling, with sweat running down his face. She tried to stroke his neck but he moved away from her.

'Should I send for a doctor?'

'Bella,' he said. 'Bella, Bella.'

'Try to relax,' she said. 'Try to think about something pretty. Flowers, or something. Try for the boy's sake.'

'Bella,' he said. 'Bella, Bella.'

When she woke up the next morning he was still crouching there in that dark corner gripping his hands together tight, and he wouldn't eat or speak—not even to the boy.

The living-room was in a mess, papers spilled everywhere, as if he had been searching for something.

Finally—it must have been around noon—he put on his hat and walked out of the house. She knew right then that she should have stopped him. That she shouldn't have let him go. She knew.

Her father came around at five o'clock and she could tell from the expression on his face that she had guessed right. Mr and Mrs Garber were with him.

'He's dead?' Bella asked.

'Shapiro's boy, the doctor,' Mr Garber said, 'said it was quick.'

'Shapiro's boy,' Mrs Garber said.

'It wasn't the driver's fault,' Mr Myerson said.

'I know,' Bella said.

Mordecai Richler

Acknowledgements

Acknowledgements are due to: Dan Davin and Robert Hale—'East is West' from *Breathing Spaces*; David Campbell and the University of Queensland Press—'Zero at Raboul' from *Flame and Shadow: Selected Stories*; Mrs. Margaret Owen Hutchinson— 'All in the Day' by R.C. Hutchinson; The Estate of the late H.E. Bates and Jonathan Cape Ltd—'There's No Future In It' from *The Stories of Flying Officer 'X'*; Thomas Raddel and McClelland and Stewart Ltd— 'Silk for Lennie' from *A Master of Arms*; 'The Enthusiastic Prisoner' by E.O. Schlunke from *Stories of the Riverina* selected by Clement Semmler. Reprinted with the permission of Angus and Robertson Publishers, Sydney. Copyright © D., J.A. & P. Schlunke.

Every effort has been made to trace owners of copyright but in some cases this has not proved possible. The publishers would be glad to hear from any further copyright owners of material reproduction in *A Time to Fight*.

Other Getaway Books

A Walk to See the King
Rony Robinson

Will and Martha might well have lived and died in
their Kent village without ever leaving it. But 1381
was the year of the great protest march. The year of
the Mad Priest. And the year of the scarred old soldier
—Wat Tyler. Will and Martha found their lives
caught up in the Walk. Separated, they are swept along
to London, and the King. They come to know that
the Walk cannot end happily for both Tyler and King,
or Will and Martha . . .

In 1381 Britain was a violent country, rigidly divided
between rich and poor. Instant justice was handed
down by whoever was in control, be it the King's army
or, momentarily, Wat Tyler's rabble. This novel
accurately reflects that world in a robust, exciting and
often moving account of two lives carried along on the
flood tide of a nation's anger, contrasted with the
struggle of a young King to assert himself as a person
instead of a symbol.